The Little Book on

Getting Started as an Expert Witness

The Little Book on

Getting Started as an Expert Witness

Chris Pamplin PhD and Susanne White PhD
UK Register of Expert Witnesses

J S Publications
11 Kings Court
Newmarket
Suffolk
CB8 7SG

ISBN 1-905926 04 6

First published: November 2008

Contents in Brief

Preface

Following on from the success of the first two Little Books in the series, Dr Chris Pamplin (Editor of the UK Register of Expert Witnesses) has teamed up with Dr Susanne White (writer and copy editor) to present a practical guide to getting started as an expert witness. Each draws on over 20 years' experience of working within the expert witness arena. The authors bring to the task a practical no-nonsense approach aimed at translating sometimes quite technical concepts into readable digestible material.

If you're contemplating taking on the role of expert witness, or are just starting out, then this Little Book offers lots of practical advice about building a successful expert witness business.

The guide is written in a light, highly readable format, with lots of sidebar summaries offering a content overview. It will help you to analyse your motives, explore the different roles and duties of an expert witness and decide whether this really is a good career move for you. It contains lots of background information on expert witness work, plus hints and tips about getting ready for an instruction.

Good preparation is the first part of the equation. It includes establishing an appropriate office environment, presenting a professional image, planning for professional development, establishing rigorous work mechanisms and creating a marketable service.

Next there's your relationship building abilities. Can you balance the provision of a professional expert witness service with the timely collection of your fee? You must foster respectful and productive work relationships that can also accommodate, when necessary, the hard-nosed businessman.

Get both right, and jobs will start to flow in from repeat work and personal recommendation. But there's much more you can do to increase your rate of instruction, and the book offers lots of suggestions on that topic too!

Chris Pamplin and Susanne White

Guide to abbreviations

CDPA............ Copyright, Designs and Patents Act
CFA .... conditional fee arrangements
CJC .... Civil Justice Council
CPR.............. Civil Procedure Rules
CPS .... Crown Prosecution Service
CrimPR .... Criminal Procedure Rules
ENE .... Early Neutral Evaluation
HMRC........... Her Majesty's Revenue and Customs
LSC .... Legal Services Commission
MoJ .... Ministry of Justice; formerly the Department for Constitutional Affairs, and before that the Lord Chancellor's Department
MRO .... medical reporting organisation
SJE............... single joint expert
VAT............... value added tax

Contents in Detail

1

What's it all about?

Expert witness work can be rewarding, but it isn't risk-free

Although there's no doubt that the role of the expert witness can be both personally challenging and financially rewarding, it can also be career-threatening! If you do not prepare for the task properly, offer a good level of service and comply with all the rules and regulations, you could find yourself headline news, facing discreditation, subject to costs sanctions and hauled before your professional disciplinary body to answer some difficult questions. So, it definitely pays to enter the expert witness arena with your eyes open and your groundwork done… which is where this Little Book comes in.

Are you right for this exacting role?

This first chapter offers a summary of the roles and duties required of an expert witness. We'll take a brief look at single joint experts (SJEs) and expert advisors, the qualities required of an expert witness and the nature of expert evidence. By reviewing the essential requirements and matching them to your personal strengths and weaknesses, you'll be able to make an informed decision about what you need to do to get ready for your work as an expert witness.

Good preparation leads to success

If this chapter doesn't warn you off, then in the subsequent chapters you'll learn the steps you need to take to:

- **prepare for your first instruction**
- **complete your task** competently
- **improve your chances of getting paid** on time and in full – something of interest to all expert witnesses! – and
- **build your business** into a successful expert witness practice.

For more detailed information about working as an expert witness, additional Little Book guides are available from the publisher. These include

'Expert Witness Practice in the Civil Arena' and 'Expert Witness Fees'. Surf to **www.jspubs.com/ LittleBooks** for a list of current titles or call us on 01638 561590.

1.1 What is an expert witness?

Let us start by defining the terms 'expert' and 'expert witness'.

An expert witness makes his knowledge available to the court

An **expert** can be anyone with knowledge of or experience in a particular field or discipline beyond that to be expected of a layman. An **expert witness** is an expert who makes this knowledge and experience available to a court (or other judicial or quasi-judicial bodies, e.g. tribunals, arbitrations, official enquiries, etc.) to help it understand the issues in a case and thereby reach a sound and just decision.

Moreover, an expert witness is paid for the time it takes to:

- **form an opinion** and, where necessary,
- **support that opinion** during the course of litigation.

An expert witness is paid for the time it takes to arrive at an opinion, not for the opinion itself

An expert witness is *not* paid for the opinion given, and still less for the assistance that opinion affords the client's case.

It's very important to keep these definitions clear and in focus. If you stray from acting as an expert witness into advising the client – and thus become an **expert advisor** – your immunity from suit will be removed. You must remain aware of the distinction at all times, and move into the role of expert advisor in full knowledge of the legal consequences. We'll look more closely at this issue later on (see page 19).

1.2 What is expert evidence?

Expert evidence is opinion evidence

The fundamental characteristic of expert evidence is that it is **opinion** evidence. Generally speaking, lay witnesses may give only one form of evidence, namely evidence of fact. They may not say, for example, that a vehicle was being driven recklessly, only that it ended up in the ditch. In this example...

- it is the function of the **court** (whether magistrate, judge or jury) to decide the cause of the accident based on the evidence placed before it, and
- it is the task of the **expert witness** (an accident investigator, say) to assist the court in reaching its decision with technical analysis and opinion inferred from factual evidence of, for example, skid marks.

Supporting evidence enables the court to determine the quality of opinion

To be practically of assistance to a court, however, expert evidence must also provide as much detail as is necessary to allow the court to determine whether the expert's opinions are well founded. It follows, then, that it will often include:

- **factual evidence supplied in the expert's instructions** which requires expertise in its interpretation and presentation
- **other factual evidence** which, while it may not require expertise for its comprehension, is linked inextricably to evidence that does
- **explanations of technical terms or topics**
- **hearsay evidence of a specialist nature**, e.g. as to the consensus of medical opinion on the causation of particular symptoms or conditions, as well as
- **opinions based on facts adduced** in the case.

1.3 When is expert evidence needed?

Expert evidence is needed when an issue falls outside the knowledge of the layman

Expert evidence is most obviously needed when **the evaluation of the issues requires technical or scientific knowledge only an expert in the field is likely to possess**. However, there is nothing to prevent reports for court use being commissioned on any factual matter, technical or otherwise, providing:

- it is deemed likely to be **outside the knowledge and experience of those trying the case**, and
- the **court agrees** to the evidence being called.

1.4 Admissibility

Admissibility is the control the court exerts over the expert evidence that can be adduced

Generally speaking, expert evidence is admissible whenever there are matters at issue requiring expertise for their observation, analysis or description. Moreover, the courts have customarily afforded litigants wide latitude in adducing such evidence. One reason for this is that, until the evidence has been heard, the judge has little else to go on in assessing the competence of the expert or the weight to be attached to his evidence.

The court controls the admissibility of all expert evidence

There has been some hardening of judicial attitudes on this topic, particularly so when unnecessary use of expert witnesses has resulted in delays in the hearing of cases or contributed excessively to their cost. Now the calling of expert evidence is under the **complete control of the court**.

Courts also have the power to exclude expert evidence even though it would otherwise be admissible. On the face of it, this conflicts with the right of individual litigants to present their case under conditions that do not place them at a disadvantage *vis-à-vis* their opponents – a right secured to them by the Human Rights Act 1998. Thus far, however, attempts to challenge, on human rights grounds, a court's refusal to allow parties to call the evidence they wish have met with no success (see, for example, *Daniels -v- Walker*[1]).

1.4.1 Inadmissibility

Expert evidence can be excluded for many reasons

There are a number of situations in which expert evidence might not be admissible. These include:

- if the **judge considers that the expert's qualifications or experience are not sufficiently relevant** to the issues
- if, on the proven facts of the case, the **judge can form his own conclusions** without the help of expert evidence
- **when it deals with matters that are for the judge to decide**
- **when the parties – as witnesses of fact – are capable of giving the evidence** themselves
- **when it is not produced in time** to enable parties to exchange reports within the timescale set by the court
- particularly in lower value claims, **where obtaining the expert evidence would incur a cost that is disproportionate** to the value of the claim
- when the **expert providing it fails to observe the requirements laid down by rules of court or practice directions** as to the form the report should take.

The court can reject evidence from 'hired guns'

The court also has the power, of course, to reject evidence that is otherwise admissible if it should form an unfavourable view as to the impartiality of the expert providing it.

---

1 *Daniels -v- Walker* [200] 1 *WLR* 1382.

1.5 Duties of an expert witness

Expert evidence must be truthful, thorough, honest and complete

The primary duty of an expert witness to the court is to be:

- **truthful** as to fact
- **thorough** in technical reasoning
- **honest** as to opinion and
- **complete in coverage** of relevant matters.

This applies to written reports as much as oral evidence, and regardless of whether the witness is on oath.

Expert witnesses owe a primary duty to the court and a secondary duty to those who instruct them

At the same time, when accepting instructions the expert assumes a contractual responsibility to the client:

- to **exercise due care** with regard to the investigations to be carried out, and
- to **provide opinion evidence** that is soundly based.

Many experts will assume a professional duty of care

It is also possible that an expert will assume **professional duties of care**. In many instances, these are more onerous than those that arise from contract. These duties dictate that the expert:

- undertakes only those tasks he is competent to carry out, and
- gives only those opinions he is competent to provide.

Expert witnesses must keep abreast of developments

To fulfil these duties adequately it is, of course, vital that the expert should also have kept up to date with current thinking and developments in his field.

Confidentiality is key

In addition, the expert must treat as confidential the identity of, and any information about, the client acquired in the course of investigations, unless their disclosure is required by law or has been authorised by the client.

Expert witnesses must know and abide by the rules of court

Finally, anyone accepting instructions to act as an expert witness must ensure their familiarity with the provisions of the relevant criminal or civil rules, regulations and guidance (see *Appendices 2–6*). An expert should be ever mindful of the potential consequences for the client – and himself – of a failure on his part to observe these requirements.

1.6 Roles of the expert

Experts can take on a number of distinct roles

The expert might take on a number of roles.

- When advising a party, but there is no intention of putting the expert's opinions before the court, the expert is known as an **expert advisor**.
- If the expert advisor is working 'behind the scenes' in a claim before the courts, the term **shadow expert** is often used instead.
- An expert instructed by just one party in a claim, and whose opinion is to be put before the court, is an **expert witness** proper, or **party-appointed expert**.
- If the expert witness is instructed by all the parties in a claim, then the **single joint expert** epithet applies.
- In a complex claim, involving many experts, one expert witness may be appointed the **lead expert**.
- Finally, the Civil Procedure Rules (CPR) also introduced the role of a truly court-appointed expert. Known as an **assessor**, this type of expert appointment is seldom seen in practice.

1.6.1 Expert advisor

The expert advisor is partisan

The great majority of civil cases are settled before they reach court. With many of them the role of expert may go no further than investigating the circumstances and providing the instructing solicitor with an interim report or assessment of the technical strength of the client's case. Such reports will often be used by the lawyer as a 'bargaining chip' in the negotiation that takes place with the other side.

Expert advisors do not have the immunity from suit enjoyed by expert witnesses

If the expert is involved before the case has actually begun, i.e. before the statement of claim has been served, the expert may be considered to be an 'advisory' expert rather than an expert witness. This status has important ramifications for the expert as it removes any claim to immunity against civil suit the expert may later wish to assert.

Prosecution experts in criminal cases are instructed in contemplation of litigation so are immune from suit – probably!

In criminal proceedings an expert may well be involved in the evidence gathering process before the prosecuting authority has made its decision to take the case to trial. Would he then be acting as an expert advisor?

Well, it's not absolutely clear. But it could certainly be argued that experts involved in the early stages of a criminal investigation have been instructed in contemplation of litigation. Indeed, under the rules of disclosure associated with criminal cases, once the defendant is charged, all expert evidence acquired will be available for the court and all parties to consider.

Both of these lines of argument point to the expert involved in early evidence gathering in a criminal case enjoying immunity from suit.

1.6.2 Expert witness

Expert witnesses have more duties than expert advisors

The expert's duties may be extended greatly if it should be decided to proceed to trial. The expert may then be expected to advise on:

- the **technical matters averred in the case**
- the **technical content of requests for further particulars** (or the responses to such requests), and
- the **technical significance of evidence disclosed** by the opposing side.

The expert may also be asked to produce a report for use in court. Furthermore, after reports have been exchanged, the expert will probably be asked for an assessment of the report prepared by the expert for the opposing side. He may also be required to take part in expert discussions with a view to narrowing issues still in dispute.

During the trial, an expert will not only have to face cross-examination on his own evidence, but be on hand to advise counsel about weaknesses to be probed in that of the opposing side's expert.

Finally, the expert may be required to provide further technical support should the case go to appeal.

Expert witness work often involves more than simply writing a report

It can be seen that an expert can have several distinct roles to play in litigation, that these roles will overlap in time and that they may extend over the duration of a case, from inception to appeal. Being an expert witness is not simply a matter of writing reports – it can involve much else besides.

1.6.3 Single Joint Expert

An SJE owes an overriding duty to the court

Seen most commonly in civil courts, but also of limited use in criminal cases, the SJE owes the same overriding duty to the court as any other expert.

The role an SJE performs is governed by the following provisions:

- CPR Part 35 and its associated Practice Direction
- Criminal Procedure Rule (CrimPR) Part 33
- Practice Direction: Experts in Family Proceedings relating to Children.

An SJE's duty to the parties is more complex

The SJE also owes the same duties of professional competence to the instructing parties as any expert appointed by one party alone. However, because an SJE has more than one instructing party, there is an extra requirement that in any dealings with the parties an SJE must conduct himself in a scrupulously fair and transparent manner. This places additional burdens on the SJE.

An SJE must avoid unilateral communication

- **Each party must be kept informed** of the progress being made.
- The SJE must **avoid communicating unilaterally** with any party – so telephone conversations should be avoided.

Tact and a firm resolve are the hallmarks of a good SJE

There is also the possibility that one or more of the instructing parties may have wanted to instruct their own expert but were not allowed to do so by the court. If that is the case, they might well feel prejudiced. Initially, at least, they may fail to co-operate fully with the SJE whom they and their opponents have been ordered to appoint. Tact and a firm resolve are not the least of the skills required of an SJE if the role is to be fulfilled successfully.

Party-appointed experts often feel 'part of the team'

Although the primary duty of all expert witnesses is to the court, those appointed by one party alone may still have the sense of belonging to that party's 'team'. This is especially so if they have advised on technical aspects of the case prior to the issue of proceedings.

SJEs often feel isolated

The situation of the SJE could not be more different.

- In the great majority of instances the SJE would have had **no knowledge of the case before being appointed**, and thereafter little or no influence in determining the course it takes.
- Throughout the SJE's involvement he will be expected to **maintain a position of strict neutrality** *vis-à-vis* the parties, even to the extent that should one of them make contact for any reason, the SJE would be expected to ensure that the other party/parties knows of it and has a copy of any response.
- If an SJE is required to give evidence in court, it is likely that the **instructing parties would avoid having any contact** while there. It is probable that neither side will feel in the least obliged to tell the SJE how the case is going, when the evidence is likely to be called and how long the SJE should remain in the court building.
- It is also **unlikely that either of the parties will inform the SJE subsequently of the case's outcome**.

Isolation, in a word, is a fact of life for SJEs, and not the least of its tribulations.

1.7 Qualities required of an expert witness

Expert witnesses must be independent, objective and unbiased

Expert evidence must be – and must be *seen* to be – independent, objective and unbiased. In particular, an expert witness must not be biased towards the party responsible for paying the fee. The evidence should be the same whoever is paying.

Clearly, too, an expert witness should have:

- a **sound knowledge of the subject matter** in dispute, and, usually, practical experience of it

- the **powers of analytical reasoning** required to fulfil the assignment
- the **ability to communicate findings and opinions** clearly, concisely and in terms adapted to the tribunal before which evidence is being given
- the **flexibility of mind to modify opinions** in the light of counter-arguments or fresh evidence
- the **ability to 'think on one's feet'**, so necessary in coping with cross-examination and re-examination.

1.8 Qualifications, training and accreditation

There are no prerequisites for becoming an expert witness

The courts do not require an expert to lay claim to any particular qualifications, training or accreditation as a prerequisite to admitting his evidence. It is enough for a party to demonstrate that:

- the **court will benefit from the proposed evidence**
- the evidence is **technical evidence that would not otherwise be available** to the court, and
- the **expert possesses suitable expertise**.

Experience is often more important than qualifications

While formal qualifications will help the court in assessing an expert's expertise, the expert's professional experience will often be more relevant.

Training in the duties of an expert witness makes many experts feel more confident in their interactions with lawyers and the courts. There are numerous commercial training companies and expert witness bodies that offer courses, conferences, workshops and mentoring (see §3.4.1 Training on page 62).

Mandatory accreditation of expert witnesses is undesirable

The Civil Justice Council (CJC) has concluded that mandatory accreditation of expert witnesses is neither possible nor desirable. Instead, the CJC has said that professional organisations and expert bodies should work together to implement high standards and follow principles of accreditation on which a broad consensus can be reached.

1.9 So what's your motivation?

The first question you should ask yourself is 'What is my motivation for doing this?' You may be able to respond with just one clear-cut answer. But more often there will be several factors contributing to your decision.

- You want to **earn more cash** and see expert witness work as a way of doing it.
- You are **intellectually interested** in moving into this sphere, getting to grips with the law and battling with strong legal minds.
- It has simply become a **part of your job**, an adjunct you didn't really seek.
- You want to '**do some good**' and help justice be served.

Let's take each of these factors in turn and perhaps dispel some common misconceptions on the way!

1.9.1 Earn more cash

This is not as easy as you may like to think!

What you can charge will vary depending on the paymaster

The fees you can charge will depend on who is your paymaster. You can charge privately funded clients whatever they are willing to pay. However, most clients will want to keep costs proportionate to the value of the claim. (For details of expert witness fee scales, see *Appendix 1*.) But the Legal Services Commission (LSC) has relatively strict guideline fee scales within which it will attempt to keep your fees. These scales can be consulted in *Appendix 9: MoJ*

Guidance to Determining Officers and fall well below the usual professional fees charged.

Once invoiced, you've then the added headache of encouraging your instructing solicitor to pay you in full and on time. A signed written contract is essential, as is a no-nonsense business-like approach from the outset.

Think too about the upfront costs you may incur.

- Do you have all the skills necessary to do battle in court, or will you have to fork out cash for training courses?
- How's your letterhead and promotional material looking? Tired? Dated? Will you need to tailor your letterhead and brochures to your expert witness services?
- What about your website? Do you have one? Does it need a new page or a complete revamp to accommodate this new service?
- Will your current secretarial and administrative systems cope with the new services you wish to offer? If not, what will you need to do to ensure they can cope?
- Will you need to register for VAT? If so, can you deal with VAT registration and ongoing paperwork yourself or will accountants need to get involved?
- Are your current premises capable of coping with any additional meetings you will need to hold? Are they, in fact, suitable for entertaining client meetings, or will you need to pay for ad-hoc meeting rooms elsewhere?

As you can see, there may be some considerable financial outlays required before you feel able to begin offering expert witness services.

1.9.2 Added mental stimulation

Expert witness work can prove highly stimulating, but it brings with it lots of administrative tasks

There's no doubt that the role of the expert witness can be mentally stimulating and challenging. But there's also a lot of background administrative and secretarial work involved too, like:

- **answering telephone enquiries** from lawyers and case clients
- **keeping an appointment diary**
- **checking on court times and dates**
- **photocopying reports**
- **locating essential, yet missing, documents**, and
- **issuing and chasing invoices**.

Do you have someone you can trust to take away these repetitive unskilled tasks, or will you have to do it all yourself?

Not everyone can cope with cross-examination

To stand up in court and answer questions from hostile barristers takes strong mental fibre. Are you honestly up to the task? Will you relish the combative style? Are you self-assured yet willing to listen? Can you think on your feet and not get flustered?

1.9.3 Adjunct to your job

You may need help to ensure you can communicate effectively from the witness box

If the role has been landed on you, then take some time to consider the qualities required of a successful expert witness. Do they truly match your personal strengths? If not, could the right training, support and guidance help?

There's no doubt that the role of the expert witness is not for everyone. While 98% of civil cases are paper-based projects requiring the inquisitive, analytical mind and an accurate pen, there may well come a time when the courtroom beckons and a whole new set of skills is required. Could you be an impressive expert witness in the courtroom? You will be doing yourself and your clients an injustice if you practise as an expert witness when you know your oral presentation skills are not sufficiently polished to communicate effectively in the courtroom.

1.9.4 'Do some good'

Expert witnesses are not 'white knights on silver chargers'!

It's a laudable aim. But remember, your role is to make your knowledge and experience available to a court to help it understand the issues of a case and thereby reach a sound and just decision.

- You may **have an opinion, but may not pass judgment**.
- You must **be wholly unbiased**, regardless of any personal feelings.
- You must accept that **there will be times when (in your opinion) you observe injustice** and can do nothing to prevent it occurring.
- You must **arm yourself against personal verbal attacks** of your professional standing and not take them too much to heart.

1.10 Conclusions

Go in with your eyes open and your wits about you

You must go into expert witness work with your eyes wide open. You should:

- concentrate on **providing a top-quality service**
- **ensure deadlines are met**
- **comply with all the relevant rules** and regulations
- **maintain a no-nonsense business-like manner** at all times
- **understand your weaknesses**

- **plan for personal improvement**
- invest in **creating the right image**, and
- aim to **develop long-lasting, professional relationships**.

If you can succeed in each of the above, and get your marketing right, you should create a thriving expert witness practice that will offer both mental challenge and financial reward. And most of the time you'll be 'doing good' too!

2

Justice systems in England and Wales

The justice system in England and Wales is split into civil (including family) and criminal

The legal system in England and Wales can be divided into:

- the **criminal** justice system – involving cases where the State takes action against a party to determine whether it has committed a crime
- the **civil** justice system (which includes family proceedings) – in which a party takes action against another, usually with the aim of achieving financial compensation.

Which court will hear the case and which procedures will be followed will depend on a number of factors including the nature of the charge and the consequences of a guilty or liable verdict.

The parties argue their case before the court

At most court hearings two or more parties come before the court to request a ruling. Each party is usually represented by a lawyer who argues the case. At a hearing, the court needs to:

- **find out what happened**, i.e. establish the facts
- if necessary, **call for expert opinion** to inform the court's decision
- before making a ruling, **determine applicable law**, and
- **make a ruling**.

2.1 Evidence

There are three types of evidence

There are three categories of evidence, regardless of whether the trial is civil or criminal:

- **documentary** evidence – including photographs, video and audio recordings, photofits, documents (e.g. letters, memos, e-mails, hospital records), etc.
- **real** evidence – e.g. a firearm, a signature, radar traces, photographs, video and audio recordings

- **witness** evidence – i.e. eyewitnesses, professional witnesses and expert witnesses.

2.2 Witness evidence

There are three different types of witness:

- **witness of fact** (eyewitness) – someone who observed or heard something during an incident and can give evidence about what happened, but must not give an opinion, e.g. an eyewitness to a road traffic accident. A statement is given, and an appearance at court is not required unless the parties fail to agree that the statement can be read in court.

Eyewitnesses report what they saw happen

- **professional witness** – a professional who saw something happen in the course of their everyday job, e.g. police officers, police surgeons or a nurse who saw a patient and recorded injury details. They mainly give factual evidence, but can offer some opinion. A statement is made and, if the statement is not disputed, a court appearance will be unnecessary.

Professional witnesses give technical evidence about what they saw in their line of work

- **expert witness** – a professional called to give expert opinion based on the facts (assumed or observed) of a case. An expert witness will write a report and will be asked to attend court if any party wishes to hear his oral evidence or conduct a cross-examination of his evidence.

Expert witnesses give opinions based on evidence they are asked to consider

2.3 Disclosure

Disclosure of evidence refers to the act of informing all opposing parties of the evidence held.

In civil litigation, full disclosure is encouraged to help parties reach an early settlement, thus decreasing costs.

Disclosure is a matter for the lawyers, but the wise expert will understand the basics anyway!

In family proceedings, if a party commissions a report from an expert witness, the report must be disclosed to the judge and all other parties, regardless of its content. There are no exceptions.

In criminal litigation, disclosure ensures that parties cannot be ambushed at trial with previously unannounced evidence or witnesses. Expert evidence that is not disclosed until trial will almost certainly be ruled inadmissible.

2.4 Civil proceedings

Most civil cases never reach trial

Some 96% of civil litigation cases settle before they reach trial. Of the remaining 4% of cases, they are all started in either the county court or the High Court.

The statement of case sets out each party's claim

Civil litigation occurs between a claimant (or claimants), a defendant (or defendants) and, in some cases, other parties. Each party sets out its case in writing in a **statement of case**. A statement of case:

- **gives details of what is claimed** to have happened
- **makes allegations** against the other party(ies)
- **highlights any points of law in dispute**
- **outlines the evidence**, and
- in the case of the claimant, **defines the remedy** being claimed (usually monetary damages).

The claimant must prove liability, causation and fairness of claimed compensation

A claimant must show in court:

- that **the defendant(s) is liable** in law, i.e. is responsible for the claimant's loss or damage
- **causation**, i.e. that the defendant's actions caused the claimant's loss, and
- if liability and causation can be proved, that the **amount of money claimed (the quantum) will**

fairly compensate (as much as money can) the claimant for the loss.

In personal injury and medical negligence cases, the court will also need evidence of the current condition of the injured party and a prognosis for future recovery.

Medical cases also require condition and prognosis evidence

An expert witness can be instructed to give an opinion on liability, causation, condition and prognosis, and quantum, or a combination of some or all of these.

A person or organisation from whom money (damages) or an alternative remedy is claimed is called the defendant. A losing defendant is not found guilty, but is held liable to the claimant. Often, the 'real' defendant in a civil case will be an insurance company.

Defendants in civil actions are often insurance companies

A negotiated settlement can be reached at any point in the civil litigation process, thus halting proceedings. Contractual obligations to expert witnesses are often forgotten in these negotiations, and that omission can give rise to unnecessary wrangles over cancellation fees.

Negotiation is the name of the game

2.4.1 Burden and standard of proof

In civil cases the burden of proof lies with the claimant. The claimant must prove their case on the **balance of probabilities**, i.e. more probable than not. Any counterclaim brought by the defendant must be proved by the defence team to the same degree of certainty.

Civil claimants must prove that their account of events is more likely than not

2.4.2 Expert evidence

In civil proceedings, expert evidence is restricted by the court to that which is **reasonably required to resolve the proceedings**. In addition:

Expert evidence is under the complete control of the court

- Experts must help the court only on the matters **within their expertise**.
- Due to cost restrictions, expert evidence is **usually restricted to a written report**. Oral evidence can only be given with the court's permission.
- **Written questions may be put to experts for clarification only**. Answers will form part of the expert report.
- **SJEs are strongly encouraged**. This role brings with it new obligations for the expert.

Expert witnesses must comply with CPR Part 35

- Expert reports must **comply with the Practice Direction to Part 35** of the CPR.
- Every report must **contain a signed statement of truth** in the form prescribed by CPR Part 35.
- An expert report must **state the substance of all material instructions**, whether written or oral, on the basis of which the report was written.
- **Once disclosed, an expert report can be used as evidence by any party** to the proceedings.
- **Discussions between experts are encouraged** at the direction of the court with the aim of identifying the issues in the proceedings, reaching agreement on issues and narrowing down areas of dispute. Any agreement between experts is not binding on the parties unless the parties expressly agree to be bound by them.
- **Failure to disclose an expert report will result in the report and any consequent oral evidence from that expert being ruled inadmissible**, unless the court grants leave.

Official guidance for experts working in civil proceedings is given in:

- Part 35 of the CPR (go to www.justice.gov.uk)
- Practice Direction to CPR Part 35 (go to www.justice.gov.uk)
- CJC Experts Protocol (go to www.jspubs.com/library).

There's lots of official guidance for experts working in civil cases

2.4.3 Civil courts

County court

The county courts deal with claims involving personal injury, debt, professional negligence, contracts, building disputes, faulty goods and services and landlord and tenant disputes. Trials are open to the public.

Most civil cases start life in a county court

Exactly who presides over proceedings will depend on the value of the claim.

<£5,000	District judge
>£5,000 <£15,000	District judge, circuit judge, recorder or assistant recorder
>£15,000	Circuit judge, recorder or assistant recorder

High Court

The High Court is divided into three divisions.

- The **Family Division** hears cases that involve child welfare (including adoption), divorce and intestacy. Divorce actions are also dealt with in the county courts, and it is usually only those that involve large sums of money (or celebrity couples!) that are heard in the High Court.

The Family Division deals with child welfare and higher value divorces

- The **Chancery Division** hears claims that are principally money related, such as bankruptcy,

The Chancery Division deals with more complex money claims

land disputes, copyright, patents, company insolvency, complex wills and trusts, and equities.

Contract disputes and the like are considered by the Queen's Bench Division

- What remains is handled by the **Queen's Bench Division**, which deals with cases involving contract disputes, torts (civil wrongs) and the like. The Queen's Bench also has specialist subdivisions that hear complicated business and company cases (the **Commercial Court**), shipping cases (the **Admiralty Court**) and actions against public authorities and a variety of judicial review matters (the **Administrative Court**).

A Divisional Court hears appeals from the lower civil courts

There is also a **Divisional Court** (a court of two judges) of the High Court which sits in the Family and Chancery Divisions and hears appeals from the magistrates' and county courts.

Appeals from the High Court go to the Court of Appeal

Appeal from the High Court, once leave has been granted, lies to the **Civil Division of the Court of Appeal**, which sits at the Royal Courts of Justice.

One High Court judge usually presides over proceedings, but a circuit judge or a senior QC can also preside. A jury is involved only in cases centring around slander, libel, unlawful imprisonment or malicious prosecution.

Other courts

No new evidence can be submitted in an appeal heard by the **Court of Appeal** (Civil Division) without leave. Appeals are heard from the High Court, the county court and certain tribunals with the permission of the judge who tried the case or from the Court of Appeal. Normally three Lords Justice of Appeal sit on the bench, and they may include the Vice Chancellor, the Master of the Rolls or the Lord Chief Justice.

If there is a principle of law of great public interest, then the **House of Lords** may listen to the legal arguments. The hearing is held in a committee room of the Houses of Parliament. Usually five Lords of Appeal sit in judgment over the proceedings.

In general, **magistrates' courts** deal with criminal cases. However, they also rule upon family matters and licensing.

The magistrates' court hears family and licensing matters

2.4.4 Tracking system

All defended civil claims are allocated to one of three case management tracks:

Cases are assigned to a 'track' at an allocation hearing

- **small claims track**
- **fast track**
- **multi-track**.

Each track has different procedures and degrees of judicial management. A district judge or High Court master decides on the track at an **allocation hearing**, using information supplied by the parties in an allocation questionnaire.

Small claims track

Claims valued at <£5,000 (or £1,000 for personal injury or housing disrepair) are assigned to the small claims track. All small claims cases are heard in the county court and should be concluded within 30 weeks of track allocation.

There's limited use of expert evidence in small claims cases

Hearings are informal and can be conducted without a lawyer. The losing party is not usually ordered to pay all the winner's costs, just the court fee and witness and travelling expenses. Expert evidence is rarely permitted given the low value of the claim. If it is, then it will be in the form of a written report only.

Much of CPR 35 is waived for small claims cases

Fast track

Simple claims between £5,000 and £15,000 where the trial can be heard in 1 day or less will be assigned to the fast track. All fast track cases are heard in the county court and should be concluded within 30 weeks of track allocation.

Multi-track

Larger, or more complex, cases are dealt with on the multi-track

The multi-track is the norm for claims greater than £15,000 or for complex lower value claims. Multi-track cases will be given their own timetables, but should reach trial in 1–2 years.

The multi-track may be managed by district judges in the county court, but the trial will be heard by a circuit or High Court judge.

2.5 Family proceedings

The family justice system seeks to minimise the destructive effects of disputes

The family justice system exists to help families avoid disputes. If disputes or problems should arise, the system tries to enable them to be resolved quickly and with the minimum of pain caused to those involved. If at all possible, the parties are encouraged to resolve their disputes out of court, e.g. through mediation, because they are more likely to adhere to an agreement if they themselves have had a role in formulating it.

When disputes do come to court, the cases are dealt with by magistrates and judges who are specially trained to deal with the family-related issues. These disputes often involve very difficult and sensitive circumstances, e.g. relationship breakdown or child contact.

Family cases are far less adversarial

Judges and magistrates work to make the circumstances of the family dispute less adversarial, and hearings can often be quite informal with, for example, all parties sitting around a table. The key points for experts to remember when involved in such proceedings are openness, transparency and independence.

Experts involved in family proceedings are usually medically qualified.

Family courts mostly use medical experts

- Paediatricians may be asked to examine, for example, bruising and lacerations on a child to determine causation.
- Forensic dentists or odontologists may be asked to consider X-rays and dental injuries to determine causation.
- Psychiatrists or psychologists may be asked to assess child mental health or parenting capacity.

Other non-medical expertise required can include dieticians, social workers and educationalists.

2.5.1 Types of proceeding

Family proceedings relating to children under the Children Act 1989 are divided into three categories:

There are three types of family proceeding: private, public and adoption

- **Private** law proceedings – most commonly disputes between separated parents over their children (residency, contact, etc.)
- **Public** law proceedings – cases concerned with the temporary or permanent removal of a child from its family into the care of a local authority (the applicant)
- **Adoption** proceedings – either public or private.

The use of experts is much more common in public law proceedings.

An enquiry can come to an expert witness from a solicitor acting on behalf of:

- the parents
- the child
- the local authority

- another interested party, most usually the Children and Family Court Advisory Support Service (CAFCASS).

All care proceedings start in the Family Proceedings Court based at a magistrates' court. Complex cases involving expert evidence and other medical issues are usually transferred up to the county court or High Court.

2.5.2 Standard of proof

Family decisions are (broadly) made on the balance of probabilities

Decisions are made 'on the balance of probabilities', the same standard of proof as in other civil cases. However, 'balance' as used here is a flexible concept. Indeed, the more serious or improbable an allegation of abuse, the more convincing must be the evidence required to prove the allegation.

2.5.3 Important differences

There are three important points worth noting...

Family cases are non-adversarial, confidential and not privileged

1 The proceedings are **non-adversarial** – the court is wholly concerned with the welfare of the child or children involved in the proceedings.

2 The proceedings are **confidential**. All documents in family proceedings are confidential to the court. It is a contempt of court to disclose them to anyone not party to the proceedings without the court's permission. The judge decides what issues require expert evidence and the instructions the expert should be given.

3 Litigation **privilege does not apply**. If a party commissions a report from an expert witness, the report must be disclosed to the judge and all other parties, regardless of its content. There are no exceptions.

2.5.4 Expert evidence

Expert evidence (usually medical) is often crucial in a difficult case involving a child. Indeed, it is usually determinative of a child's future. The court places much reliance on the professional integrity of the expert witnesses.

The family court is highly dependent on the integrity of medical experts

It should be remembered that...

- the **general duties of experts in civil proceedings apply** in family proceedings

In general, all CPR apply

- the expert witness is appointed to **assist the judge** in reaching the right result for the child or children involved, regardless of the instructing party
- the expert witness owes a **duty to the court and to the child** involved in the case, not to the commissioning party
- there is **no such thing as an 'off the record' discussion** for an expert instructed in family proceedings. Anything he is told during his investigations must be reported and disclosed to the court and all the parties involved.

Nothing is ever 'off the record'

- **whatever the expert does or says will be disclosed**, e.g. attendance notes (a solicitor's note of a telephone conversation), letters, e-mails, etc.
- quite often, **criminal and family proceedings can arise from the same set of facts**, e.g. if a child has been sexually abused by a parent
- **hearsay evidence is also admissible**
- an expert is **free to give an opinion about any issue** in the case, including those that fall within the judge's remit. However, an opinion must be related to a matter that falls within the expert's area of expertise.

Uniquely, experts can give opinion on any aspect of the case

- **caution should be taken if firm opinions are expressed about events having taken place** – the expert may not have all the relevant information
- the **court is keen to avoid multiple physical or psychiatric examinations of a child** by several experts. If it allows just one examination, then only a single jointly appointed expert will be permitted.

A family-specific practice direction is now in force

A practice direction has been published (Experts in Family Proceedings relating to Children) to guide experts in family proceedings. It can be viewed on Her Majesty's Courts Service website (www.hmcourts-service.gov.uk) or in *Appendix 6*.

2.6 Criminal proceedings

In criminal cases, the State prosecutes a defendant

The bulk of criminal cases are brought against a defendant (an individual or company) by the State's prosecuting authority – the Crown Prosecution Service (CPS). Indeed, the State funds the investigation and prosecution of all criminal cases. Citizens may also bring private prosecutions which must be self-funded.

Investigations are undertaken before the prosecuting authority decides whether to proceed to trial

A criminal case begins with an investigation by, for example:

- the police
- the Revenue and Customs Prosecutions Office (RCPO)
- the Serious Fraud Office (SFO)
- a local authority
- the Department for Business, Enterprise and Regulatory Reform (BERR), or
- the Attorney General.

The prosecuting authority will work in the early stages of a case to gather evidence so that an assessment can be made as to the likelihood of a successful prosecution.

Following the investigative phase, if it is believed that a crime has been committed, then one of two courses will be followed.

1 If it is unnecessary to arrest the offender, a summons/requisition will be served on the offender advising that it is believed that he has committed a criminal offence.

2 If the defendant is to be arrested, then the police will detain, interview and charge him.

Whichever course is followed, the prosecuting authority will take the criminal proceedings forward to trial.

There are three types of offence in criminal proceedings:

There are three types of criminal proceeding: summary, indictable and either way

- **summary** – the less serious offences which are heard in the magistrates' or youth court
- **either way** – heard in either the magistrates'/ youth or the crown court, with the magistrates deciding the venue at a Mode of Trial hearing
- **indictable** – the most serious offences which are heard in the crown court.

Whichever category the case falls into, the magistrates' court or youth court will be the first port of call. The relevant court will deal itself with all summary and some either way cases, but it will commit all indictable and other either way cases to the crown court.

All criminal cases start in the magistrates' or youth court

If a defendant pleads guilty, a full trial does not go ahead; the court meets only to decide on sentencing. If a defendant pleads not guilty, a full trial proceeds.

A guilty plea stops a full trial proceeding

If found guilty, sentencing usually takes place at a later date.

Over 90% of criminal cases are disposed of in magistrates' or youth courts

All criminal cases start out life in the magistrates' or youth court, and more than 90% are disposed of there. The magistrates or a district judge need to decide:

- whether there is a **case to answer**
- whether the defendant should be held in **custody** to await trial
- whether the defendant should be offered **bail** on conditions and released, subject to him returning to court on a given date
- whether the defendant is eligible for **legal aid**, and
- the **trial court** – magistrates' or youth (summary trial) or crown (trial on indictment) court.

2.6.1 Magistrates' court/youth court

Summary cases are dealt with entirely in the magistrates' or youth court

Criminal trials completed in a magistrates' or youth court are called summary trials. They are heard by magistrates (usually three lay magistrates sit on the bench) or a district judge (who is a qualified lawyer with at least 7 years' experience). They consider the less serious crimes, e.g. speeding offences, shoplifting, minor theft, minor assault, etc.

The court needs to:

- decide whether the defendant is **guilty or not guilty**

and, if guilty:

- decide whether to **adjourn** to obtain a pre-sentence report from the Probation Service
- **pass sentence**, or

- **send the guilty party to the crown court** (which has wider sentencing powers).

The magistrates are not lawyers and have volunteered their time to sit as Justices of the Peace. They are assisted by a magistrate's clerk, who is legally qualified and advises them on matters of law.

Magistrates are not lawyers

It can quickly be seen that timetabling in the magistrates'/youth court is near impossible. The uncertain nature of the unfolding case – whether it will be a quick 15-minute 'no case to answer' session, a more lengthy full trial or something in between – means that participants can be left waiting for hours while preceding cases are handled.

Timetabling is very difficult – expect to wait around!

2.6.2 Crown court

The remaining criminal trials are heard in the crown court. This court considers the more serious offences, including murder, rape, robbery, fraud, dangerous driving, serious assault and drug offences.

The crown court deals with more serious cases

The crown court also hears:

- **appeals** from the magistrates' or youth court and
- **cases transferred** from the magistrates' or youth court for sentencing.

Crown court trials are presided over by a judge and empanel a jury. The judge may be a High Court judge, a circuit judge or a recorder. The role of the judge is to:

The judge controls the proceedings

- **control the proceedings**
- **direct the jury on the law**
- **direct the jury as to the weight to be attached to the evidence** of each witness
- **pass sentence** if the defendant is convicted.

The jury makes the decision on guilt

The role of the jury is to:

- **listen carefully** to the evidence
- **decide whether the defendant is guilty or not guilty**.

Similar timetabling problems to the magistrates' court exist in the crown court but to a greater degree. Participants can be left waiting for days for a trial to begin!

2.6.3 Appeal courts

Expert evidence is seldom admitted in the appeal courts

The appeal court structure is very complicated and does not usually apply to expert witnesses. Expert evidence will be confined almost exclusively to the magistrates', youth or crown court at the main trial hearing. The higher courts are wholly appellate, which means that they rarely consider new evidence.

Exceptions include evidence from recent breakthrough scientific techniques

The only new expert evidence that may be allowed at an appeal court would be evidence that has come to light since the original trial that could not have been available at the time. So, for example, if science has progressed rapidly and a new forensic science technique has been developed, the application of which has provided new evidence, then that may be allowed.

2.6.4 Burden and standard of proof

Case must be proved beyond reasonable doubt

In general, the prosecuting authority has to prove its case, showing that there is sufficient evidence to find the defendant guilty. To secure a conviction, the prosecuting authority must prove **beyond reasonable doubt** every element of their case.

Burden of proof can switch to the defence in some situations

In a few instances the burden of proof falls on the defence team, e.g. if the defendant wishes to plead insanity or diminished responsibility. However, in this case the defence team is only required to prove on the balance of probability rather than beyond reasonable doubt.

2.6.5 Expert evidence

CrimPR 33 governs experts in criminal cases

Expert evidence in criminal trials is governed by Part 33 of the CrimPR. They can be viewed through the Ministry of Justice (MoJ) website at www.justice.gov.uk. In brief...

- An expert must p**rovide objective, unbiased opinion on matters within his expertise**.
- An expert must **inform all parties and the court if his opinion changes** from that contained in his report.
- **Pre-hearing discussions of expert evidence are encouraged** to determine areas of agreement and narrow areas of disagreement.
- **Expert evidence cannot be admitted without the court's permission**.
- **SJEs can only be appointed between defendants**.

CPS publishes guidance for prosecution experts

Further guidance is offered to prosecution experts by the CPS in Chapters 36 and 37 and Annex K of their Disclosure Manual (Disclosure: Experts' evidence and unused material – Guidance Booklet for Experts). It can be viewed on-line in full through the website of the CPS (www.cps.gov.uk) or through the 'Expert Library' of the *UK Register of Expert Witnesses* at www.jspubs.com.

3

Preparing your service

Get the basics in place before offering your services

This chapter takes you briefly through a lot of the essentials that should be in place before you seek that first instruction. If you are already in business, then much of what follows may well have been addressed already. But it's worth a quick skim through to ensure you haven't missed anything.

Invest time now to help your business flourish

So, before embarking on your first instruction it is vital that you prepare your business environment. Successful completion of a first instruction is most likely to be achieved if you have put in the groundwork to get the business basics right. By posing important questions, what follows will help you to think about how each business basic affects you.

The necessary preparations will take you a little time, but it is essential to put the effort in now if you wish this sort of work to grow and to generate an income in the years to come.

3.1 Office

Make sure your office set up gives the right impression

It's important that your office environment sets a professional tone in every respect, be it the decoration, the way your telephones are answered or the efficiency of your staff. You should examine every point of interaction between a client and your business, and then decide whether your business presentation is up to scratch.

3.1.1 Office building

Can you hold private meetings at your office?

Most of your clients will never meet you face to face; if they do, it will be at their offices or in a court building. On occasions, though, you may need to host a meeting.

- **Can you receive clients or hold expert discussions at your office?** If your office is not suitable for such confidential meetings, scout around the local area and pinpoint better premises for occasional hire. Try hotels, schools, universities and colleges, conference centres, and so on.

- **Is your office fully accessible** to people of all abilities?

3.1.2 Mail

It's the nature of expert witness work that there is usually a great deal of associated paperwork, some of it confidential.

How capable is your office of swiftly handling confidential mail?

- **Can your office receive large bundles of post during work hours?**
- Some documents will be confidential. **Do you have a secure fire-safe place to store sensitive material**?
- **Are you in the office daily to check your post?**
- If important documents arrive while you are away, **is there a system in place to forward documents to you?**

An alternative postal system to Royal Mail is Document Exchange, or 'The DX'. Heavily used by law firms, it offers a more secure postal service for next day business mail. Go to www.thedx.co.uk for more information.

For post leaving your office…

- Do you have an easily accessible **local post office** you can use to weigh and stamp your mail?
- Will postage stamps suffice, or will you need to invest in **franking equipment** and weighing scales?

NB The Royal Mail is now quite vigilant in imposing financial penalties for wrongly stamped mail, be

Make sure you get the postage right

it on the sending or the receiving party. And this penalty process also results in delays to the mail and disgruntled clients.

3.1.3 Address

Does the business address create the desired impression?

For some businesses the location of the contact address goes towards creating the right company image – it sets the professional tone. For example, a Harley Street, London address is associated with top-flight medical consultants.

- If you work from home, **do you need to consider an alternative business address** – for security, postal collection or secretarial support reasons?

Use a PO Box to mask your home address

One possibility is to ask the Post Office for a PO Box number (prices start at £60.15 in 2008). You can then either pick up the post from your PO Box or pay an additional fee for it to be delivered to an alternative address. Any mail requiring a signature will be kept at the post office and an advice card placed in your PO Box. It will take approximately 10 days for the Post Office to set up this service for you. Go to www.royalmail.com for further information.

Alternatively, you could use a **commercial messaging service** that will:

- **receive your post** at their address
- **forward mail** to your preferred address
- **answer your telephone** calls, and
- **forward messages** to you.

There are many commercial messaging services available. A specialised expert witness service is offered by J S Publications. Call 01638 561590 for more details.

3.1.4 Telephone answering service

For most prospective clients the first point of contact with you will be your telephone answering system – be it manned or automatic.

All telephone calls must be answered professionally, ideally in person

- **Can you reliably be contacted by telephone during work hours?**
- **Can your current staff cope with the extra work?**
- Will an **answerphone** create the right impression? Will you remember to check it regularly?
- If a **home telephone number**, will you need to brief family members on how to answer the telephone?
- Should you consider a **professional telephone messaging service**? – see §3.1.3 for more details.

If you are often out and about, consider a messaging service

3.1.5 Facsimile, scanner, photocopier, etc.

The range of new business technology you'll need to acquire will depend on your current business set up.

Will your current office equipment meet your needs?

- Do you need a **fax machine** or will **e-mail** attachments suffice?
- Do you need to **scan** material or would you use a **bureau** instead?
- Do you need to hire a **photocopier**, or can you get your material photocopied elsewhere? Remember that some of the paperwork you may need copying will be confidential. Using a bureau for this work may not be appropriate.

3.1.6 Software

Spend some time investigating the software options for report writing.

Take time to understand your software requirements

- Choosing a commonly available **word-processing package**, like Microsoft Word, will mean that technical assistance will be more readily available from family, friends and work colleagues.

Be wary of software claiming to write reports for you

- **Bespoke report writing software** is available too. The simple completion of a few tick box forms and the input of a small amount of original writing results in the generation of a report. However, automation of report writing is not to be encouraged. It would be difficult to apply the same level of thought and analysis to an automated process than to a wholly original creation.

Building your own template report is well worth the effort

- **Spend time preparing an empty report template** with the standard repeated sections and styles set up. Use it as the starting point for reports; anything more automated should be treated with due caution.
- **Think about what you need the software to be able to do**. For example, how well will it cope with indexing, tables, images, paragraph numbering, etc?

3.1.7 E-mail

For a small cost, register a dedicated e-mail address

Nowadays an e-mail account is an essential business tool. It offers immediate direct contact with clients wherever you are worldwide. And if you use a Blackberry or similar portable technology, you can have e-mails forwarded to you immediately and judge for yourself how quickly to respond.

- Should you set up a **dedicated e-mail account** for your expert witness work?

3.2 Personal image

Self-presentation is more important than skill when it comes to marketing

However unfair, it should be noted that **promoting your services is about 80% appearance or**

presentation and 20% knowledge or skill. With this in mind, great care should be taken to create a favourable impression whenever a prospective client is approached.

3.2.1 Website

While not essential, running a competently constructed website does create a sense that your business is one of some substance.

Do you need a shop window on-line?

- Use the site to **maintain your current CV, detail your work and provide a photograph or video/ audio clip**.
- **Keep the number of pages to a minimum** so that maintaining currency of the information is a menial task.
- Try to **find a web solution that you can update easily yourself**.
- **Write your website content carefully**. Ensure that there are no spelling or grammatical errors. Craft your text so that there is the minimum of updating required. For example, write 'Began expert witness work in 1994' rather than '14 years' experience of expert witness work'. The latter will require amending each year.
- Make sure that **each web page fits within an average screen size and that the text size can be read easily**.

Avoid adding date-sensitive material to your website

But be warned: your website must be well designed and properly implemented. A site with poor design and broken links is a liability and may drive away potential clients.

A poor website is much worse than no website at all!

3.2.2 Photographs

Add a good-quality portrait photograph to your CV and website

How you look is very important, particularly in the courtroom. While you do not need to seek the help of a personal stylist and professional photographer to obtain the perfect shot, a well-lit and poised portrait photograph is a useful addition to a CV, website or promotional material. It also helps lawyers to know what you look like in advance of a meeting.

3.2.3 Expert witness-specific CV

CVs must be accurate – or they will provide ammunition for the opposing side

Many experts revisit their CVs and create a specific version for lawyers that can also be appended to an expert report or marketing letter.

- **Make the layout clear and simple**.
- **Ensure every fact is wholly accurate**. Any error in your CV can potentially be exploited by opponents and portrayed as a blatant lie, thus damaging your credibility.

3.2.4 Letterhead and envelopes

A clear and sober business image is what's needed

A clear, well laid out letterhead speaks volumes, and your approach will depend on budget constraints.

- Stick to **white, cream or very light grey paper** to aid with photocopying.
- Remember that any **subtle colours or shading** in your design will probably disappear when photocopies are made.
- You do not need to go to the expense of using **colour**.
- You do not need to use a **professional design company** and print thousands of letterhead in advance.
- If you're on a tight budget, **find a letterhead you think has created a good impression for someone else** (try leafing through past correspondence files). Then have a go at copying

its layout, font styles and relative font sizes in your word processing package.

- **Place the letterhead layout in the page header and/or footer** so that it repeats accurately in the same place on the page.
- Remember to design the page so that **any typed address falls in the window of the envelopes** you use.

Don't forget that you can also **personalise your envelopes**.

- If you are going to the expense of producing printed envelopes, include a **return address**.
- As an alternative, if you use a modern franking machine, you may be able to include on the printing plate a return address and/or **corporate logo**.

3.2.5 Written letters

Aim to create the right impression with all written work

The quickest way to lose a prospective customer's interest is to write a poorly phrased letter replete with spelling errors and inconsistencies. At the end of the day you're touting for expert witness business. So make sure your letter reflects the way you write your reports – concise, measured, structured and professional.

- **Choose an easy-to-read font style and font size** for your letters and stick to it for all correspondence.
- **Work out how to use style sheets** in your word processing package to ensure you maintain consistency.
- **Carefully check grammar, spelling and punctuation** to maintain a professional image.

3.2.6 Printed promotional material

Printed promotional material is not essential; if done, it must be impressive!

Your attitude towards producing glossy promotional material will depend on your budget and the strategies adopted by your competitors.

For example, if your expertise is offered mainly by individuals, it is unlikely that many will go to the expense of producing glossy brochures. So, you could either make yourself stand out from the crowd by going to the added expense of producing professionally designed advertising material, or you may feel under less pressure to spend the money because no one else does.

Printed promotional material is not essential if you have a good letterhead and coherent and well thought out letters, or a competent website ready to explain and promote your service.

- If you do wish to produce a leaflet or brochure, **get a professional design company involved** – unless you possess highly proficient publishing skills.
- **Poorly presented printed material will harm your professional image** more than having no material at all.

3.2.7 Report presentation

The written report is at the core of expert witness work

The mainstay of expert witness work is the written report. It should be clear, concise and well structured.

- Get to know your report preparation software intimately. A little time spent now mastering **style sheets and formatting** will help to create consistently presented and easy-to-read reports.
- Create a **standard template** with repeated sections in position, like contact details, qualifications, CV, statement of truth, etc.

- Invest in a **laser printer**. Dot-matrix and ink-jet printers are perceived as old-fashioned. Their output is less stable (the ink will run if the paper gets wet) and is much less easily photocopied.

Always use a laser printer for crisp and stable output

- Will your report ever need to include **colour images**? If it does, you'll need to think about how you will reproduce your final report. Will you invest in a quality colour laser printer or will you use a bureau?
- Think about how, and indeed if, you will **bind your reports**. Investigate ease of use and relative costs.

3.3 Financial considerations

Smooth cashflow requires good 'back-office' systems

For most experts, one of the main reasons for undertaking expert witness work will be the financial rewards. But you can't invoice unless you have accurate supporting documentation, and you can't chase debts if you have a poor follow up system. What's more, you can't expect hassle-free payment unless you are working under a signed contract, the scale of the bill is expected and you chase payment as soon as it falls overdue.

3.3.1 Time management

Accurate record-keeping is the key

You can only justifiably bill for recorded time spent on a case. So accurate records are essential.

- Decide how you are going to **accurately record the work done** on a case. You will inevitably revisit cases and will need to record time spent on multiple occasions. How best can this be done?
- Remember, you will need to record sufficient detail of the work done at each stage should evidence be required to justify your bills.

3.3.2 Accounts

Invoices should be clear and accurate; they must not come as a surprise to the client

You must invoice clients on time, and bills should be clear and accurate. They should contain no surprises for the payee.

- On an ongoing basis, how will you know when the outstanding bill for a case is approaching the **agreed fee limit**? Remember, once this limit is reached, do not plough on with further work until you have spoken with your instructing solicitor. Keep everyone appraised of ongoing costs to minimise payment problems.
- How will you be reminded when **invoices fall overdue**?

Get your debt chasing system in place now

- Think about how you will **chase payment** if it becomes necessary. Do you feel comfortable doing so? If not, who can do this for you?

3.3.3 Debt chasing

Keep regular checks on each client's payment record

During your career as an expert witness you will inevitably come across bad debtors. Spend some time now thinking about the best way for you to collect these debts.

- How will you address the problem?
- Will you use a **debt collection agency**? If so, locate a good one now.
- Will you make a **small claim** through the courts?

Once you have a bad experience with a lawyer or a firm, learn from it. Was it your fault? Did you fail to keep them informed of progress and a growing bill?

Consider payment on account for known bad payers

If the fault lies squarely with the lawyer or firm, either refuse further work from them or next time demand an up-front payment.

3.3.4 Terms and conditions

A written set of terms is the bedrock of any expert business

Spend time now generating a relevant set of terms and conditions. If you are currently listed with the *UK Register of Expert Witnesses*, go to www.jspubs.com and use the on-line Terminator as a starting point. Alternatively, a Terms of Engagement Framework is reproduced in *Appendix 7*.

You'll need to think about your obligations and your:

- **report writing fees**
- **court attendance fees**
- **cancellation fees**, and
- **disbursements**.

Get your template contract checked by a lawyer

It is always worth getting your final contract checked by a lawyer before using it. Lots more detail on creating a set of terms can be found in *Expert Witness Fees*, another book in this series.

3.3.5 VAT

Exceed the VAT registration threshold and you'll need to register for VAT

Do you need to register for VAT? If your total rolling turnover of taxable supplies in any 12 month period exceeds the current VAT registration threshold (£67,000 in 2008; go to www.hmrc.gov.uk/vat/index.htm for the current figure, updated annually on 1 April), then you will need to register. This means that all your invoices must have VAT added, which can be reclaimed by your clients if they are VAT registered too. (For more detail on VAT, go to §8.1 on page 172.)

3.3.6 Charging interest

You have a statutory right to claim interest on late payments

Once an invoice falls overdue then, in part subject to your contract, you can apply interest to the outstanding amount. However, you may feel that an initially less aggressive approach is worth taking before resorting to financial penalties for late payment. You'll need to balance your desire for repeat instructions with your need for immediate payment of your bill.

And you can add a fixed sum penalty!

- When your invoices fall overdue, will you charge interest? If so, at what rate? You can refer to one of two Acts that relate to interest charges. The **Late Payments of Commercial Debts (Interest) Act 1998** provides for **interest of 8% above the current Bank of England dealing rate** (the 'reference rate') at the time the debt arose. So, if the reference rate is 4%, you are entitled to charge interest at 12%. Furthermore, the **Late Payment of Commercial Debts Regulations (2002)** amends the former Act and defines an **additional fixed sum penalty** (£40 for a debt less than £1,000; £70 for a debt of £1,000 or more but less than £10,000, and so on) that can be applied. In contrast, the **County Courts Act** provides for interest to be charged **at the rate of 8%**.

Use your contract to reinforce your statutory rights

- Set out the basis upon which interest will be applied within your terms of engagement.

3.4 Professional development

Attendance at a training course/conference and/or involvement in running expert witness organisations does not guarantee the instructing lawyer a competent expert. But it does show that you are investing your time and money in self-improvement and increasing your understanding of the expert witness regime.

3.4.1 Training

Training is not mandatory, but many experts find it helpful

While training is not required by law, there are a number of expert witness training companies and organisations currently running courses on different aspects of expert witness work. Some experts find that attending such courses improves their confidence.

However, you should always bear in mind the difference between training and coaching. For example, at no time should you let anyone tell you *what* you should be saying in court – that would be coaching and is strictly prohibited. Courtroom training should consider only court familiarisation and *how* to say what you need to say.

WARNING: Coaching is prohibited

Expert witness conferences, training courses and learning materials are currently offered by the following organisations:

Use books, conferences and courses to improve your understanding

- **J S Publications**
  www.jspubs.com
  Publisher and membership body that offers lots of useful information for expert witnesses, including books, factsheets, newsletter and e-wires. Also runs a support helpline for its members and publishes the *UK Register of Expert Witnesses*, the UK's largest expert witness directory. Contact J S Publications, PO Box 505, Newmarket, Suffolk, CB8 7TF. Tel 01638 561590.
- **Society of Expert Witnesses**
  www.sew.org.uk
  Membership body that organises two conferences annually plus training sessions for members and non-members. Also runs a helpline and mentoring scheme for its members. For further details contact the Society of Expert Witnesses at PO Box 345, Newmarket, Suffolk, CB8 7TU Tel 0845 702 3014.
- **Bond Solon Training**
  www.bondsolon.com
  Expert witness training provider. Also organises annual expert witness conference. For further

details call 020 7253 7053 or write to Bond Solon at 13 Britton Street, London, EC1M 5SX.

- **Academy of Experts**
  www.academy-experts.org
  Expert witness training provider and membership body. Organises training courses and seminars for members and non-members. For further details contact the Academy on 020 7430 0333, or at 3 Gray's Inn Square, London, WC1R 5AH.
- **Expert Witness Institute**
  www.ewi.org.uk
  Expert witness training provider and membership body. Organises training courses and seminars for members and non-members. Further details can be obtained from the Institute on 0870 366 6367, or at 1st Floor, 7 Warwick Court, London, WC1R 5DJ.
- **Professional Solutions Ltd**
  www.prosols.uk.com
  Expert witness training provider. For further details contact Janette Gulleford on 0800 195 0951 or at The Dutch House, 307–308 High Holborn, London, WC1V 7LL.
- **InPractice**
  www.inpracticetraining.com
  Specialist expert witness training provider for the healthcare sector. For further details call 020 7227 7489 or write to 5 Great College Street, Westminster, London, SW1P 3SJ.

3.4.2 Mentoring

One-to-one mentoring is very effective

Before you take on the role of expert witness or whilst immersed in a case you may wish to seek advice from colleagues with experience in the field.

- Contact your professional bodies – they may have expert witness focus groups that could help.

- The Society of Expert Witnesses offers a **mentoring scheme** that puts novice experts in direct touch with experienced expert witnesses for advice and support. Go to www.sew.org.uk for further information or call 0845 702 3014.

3.4.3 Membership of expert bodies

There are a number of organisations with expert witnesses as members, each with slightly different aims. Between them they offer conferences, training, mentoring and networking opportunities. For contact details, see §3.4.1 Training above.

For published materials relating to expert witness work, contact J S Publications at www.jspubs.com or call 01638 561590.

Other professional bodies have organised expert witness focus groups within their membership. Contact your membership bodies and ask if they have any such groups arranged.

3.5 Other important considerations

3.5.1 Professional indemnity insurance

Many experts think that cover to pay defence costs is prudent

You'll be aware of the need to insure yourself against the risk of negligence in the performance of your professional duties. But expert witness work carries its own additional risks.

Whilst expert witnesses enjoy wide-ranging protection from civil action for damages arising from their expert witness work, many still draw comfort from having professional indemnity insurance in place – if only to deal with the cost of getting rid of a vexatious action brought against them.

- Check that your current policy covers you for expert witness work. If not, buy the cover to protect yourself.

- Double-check the **exclusions** on policies. Some specifically exclude work undertaken in the USA, an altogether more litigious society.

3.5.2 Geographical coverage

How far are you willing to travel for your expert witness work?

Your expert witness work could take you all over the world. But how does this fit in with your family life and other commitments? Some experts are happy to travel the globe, while others prefer English-speaking countries, just the UK or even, for example, 'within 50 miles of York'. Decide on your geographical range now so that there is no confusion.

3.5.3 Travel planning

Whether it's a 50-mile trip to the next county or a flight to Asia, you'll need to know how you are going to travel.

- Find the best **websites for booking tickets** for air, coach or rail journeys.
- Assimilate a list of helpful **travel agents**.
- Write down in one place all your **useful telephone numbers** for taxis, National Rail Enquiries, coach travel, hire car companies and so on, and keep it with you when you travel.
- You may also need to book accommodation. Gather together details of **hotel chains** and reliable **accommodation booking websites**.

Make efforts to minimise travel and subsistence costs

Remember, though, that the courts want experts to minimise travel and overnight costs. Check the current permitted allowances to ensure you stay within budget. In general, you will need to book the cheapest fares and rooms, and avoid taxis for long journeys.

3.5.4 Client management and data protection

It is much cheaper to retain a client than to find a new one

You may want to keep in regular contact with your current clients via mailshots or newsletters:

- to remind them that you are **available for further work**
- to confirm in their minds your **eminence** as an expert witness
- to inform them that you can now offer **additional services**, or
- to advise them of **new contact details**, and so on.

Basic data management, in accordance with the Data Protection Regulations, is all it takes

To do so, you'll need to:

- **decide what information to collect** and how best to store it for future use
- **gather information** about your client contacts (current and potential) in a database or spreadsheet, and
- **merge the data** with a letter or similar promotional material.

Can you make the time for this important task, or do you have support staff who can take it on?

Whenever you gather details about people, be they lawyers or litigants, you will need to ensure you comply with the Data Protection Act.

Almost all experts will need to be registered with the Information Commissioner. You can read all about this on the Information Commissioner's website at www.ico.gov.uk. Once registered, you should make yourself aware of the eight data protection principles. These are reproduced in *Appendix 10*.

Whenever you handle information about an individual you will be processing personal data. So:

- if it is 'personal data', you must meet one of the conditions from schedule 2 of the Data Protection Act
- if it is 'sensitive personal data' (which is often the case for medical experts), you must meet conditions from schedules 2 and 3.

Browse to www.opsi.gov.uk to find the text of the Data Protection Act 1998 and its associated schedules.

3.5.5 Working partners

An expert must not stray outside his area of expertise

An expert witness must never stray outside his area of expertise. On occasions this may mean working in close collaboration with other expert witnesses who possess the 'missing' expertise.

- Can you envisage needing the help of another expert witness to complete a job? If so, think about the possible areas of skill required and investigate likely working partners.
- During your investigations, make sure that the other expert witnesses in associated fields know of your existence and availability for work. Just as you may need their help, they may come to need yours!

3.5.6 Know your competitors

Understand the competitive situation specific to your business

Your competitors are all the other experts who possess your expertise and may be called upon to give evidence in a case that would suit you. How they manage their expert witness business *and* how they market themselves to lawyers should be of great interest to you.

So, can you find out anything useful?

- Do they generally **separate their expert witness work** from their other work? If so, how?

- Do they **employ different staff** to deal with their expert witness work? For example, many medical doctors employ medico-legal secretaries to deal with all the appointments and paperwork associated with their expert witness work.
- Do they **have separate premises for their expert witness work**? For example, many medical doctors use private consulting rooms for all their expert witness consultations.
- Can you **find out their fee rates**?
- Can you elicit from them any **information about bad payers, agencies to avoid**, and so on?
- Can you get hold of **copies of their CVs**? If so, you'll be able to see how your professional experience matches against theirs.

While you are making enquiries, remember, too, to think about how your competitors are **marketing** their services.

- Have most of them invested in promotional material? If so, try to obtain copies for later scrutiny.
- Do most of them have websites? If so, take time to study them.
- How do they set themselves apart from their competitors?

3.6 Expert fees

How will you decide where to pitch your fee?

- J S Publications publishes a **biannual expert witness fee survey**. By consulting the statistics you'll be given the best available advice about average fees and fee ranges. See *Appendix 1* for details of the most recent survey.

Biannual fee statistics available from the *UK Register of Expert Witnesses*

- **Ask your professional body** for any information it may publish about fee rates.
- **Ask colleagues** to let you have details of their fee rates.
- **Look on websites** of other expert witnesses to see if their fees are advertised on-line.

Think about how you will structure your fees

How will you structure your fees?

- Will you charge an **hourly rate** for report writing, or can you offer a **fixed fee** per instruction?
- What are your **costs for secretarial work** such as photocopying?
- How will you structure fees that become due because a court hearing is **cancelled**?
- What will you charge for **attending court**?
- Will you offer **discounts** for prompt payment?

What you can charge is a market decision

You are free to set your own rates. However, you should bear in mind the following when trying to pitch your fee.

- Experienced experts with references can charge more because they are a safer bet for a solicitor. They understand how the various legal systems work, and the flow of their instruction should be generally trouble-free.
- Experts recognised as being at the top of their field will be able to charge more for their time.
- Experts in unusual areas of expertise will be instructed less frequently but can charge more per occasion.
- Experienced experts are likely to be busier. They will generally take longer to complete assignments. A solicitor needing a report quickly will probably be more inclined to consider

instructing a 'new' expert, even if some hand holding will be required.

- If your local area has a lot of experts in your discipline, then there may be more competition for local instructions. Keen pricing or ready availability may give you the edge.

The fee rate you can achieve will also be affected by:

Civil cases pay better than criminal cases

- the justice system in which you are working, i.e. civil or criminal, and
- your paymaster, e.g. CPS, LSC.

In general, civil cases will pay better than criminal cases, and private clients will pay more than the public purse. For more detail about expert fees in civil and criminal proceedings, read chapter 7.

Much more detail about expert fees is contained in another book in this series: *Expert Witness Fees*.

4

Getting instructions and growing your business

Find the right marketing mix to match your time and finances

Whether you're trying to gain a first instruction or to grow your business, this chapter will give you lots of ideas about how to proceed. There are several approaches worth trying, each with its own advantages and disadvantages. Some will require significant time and effort on your part, while others will make demands on your purse. Your task will be to find the right marketing mix to match your financial and time constraints.

Your reason for doing expert witness work will influence your strategy

Another point to consider is how you view your expert witness work. Is it something in which you want to dabble to fill the odd afternoon now and then? Or is it a new strand to your business that you are keen to strengthen and grow?

And finally, think about how your competitors market themselves. Do they all produce glossy brochures and have snazzy websites? If so, you'll need to seriously consider matching, if not exceeding, their efforts or risk being viewed as less professional. Remember, how you portray yourself is much more important at first contact than the expertise you possess.

Some of the approaches discussed below are more likely to lead to short-term gain but little long-term security. Others may take longer to produce results, but the quality of the contacts and the implications for your future success will be enhanced greatly.

Balance financial costs with effort to select the best approach for you

Low cost, low effort

- Register as an expert witness with your **professional bodies**
- Gain **word-of-mouth recommendations** from professional colleagues
- Talk to your **local law societies** and see if you can do something together of mutual benefit

Low cost, high effort

- Try to get asked for comment by **local and national TV, radio and newspapers**
- Write articles for **professional journals, newsletters and newspapers**
- Offer to give **talks and presentations** at conferences and other public events

Variable cost, low effort

- Gain an entry in an **expert witness directory** or directories
- Register with a **middleman agency**
- Advertise in the **legal press**

High cost, high effort

- Undertake a **targeted direct mailshot** to lawyers
- Join with other legal service providers in a **targeted shared mailshot** to lawyers
- Take a stand at a **legal conference** and try to inform lawyers directly

Marketing is a process – expect to revisit your strategy regularly

You will need to allow yourself time every few months to revisit each suggestion and decide whether a new strategy is now required given your current situation. For example, if you find yourself with less time for expert witness work, then perhaps you will want to stop advertising for a while, relying on 'old sales leads' to drip feed irregular work. Or maybe you've decided to start your own consultancy and are now really keen to expand quickly. You've now got lots of time but not too much cash. Which strategies now best fit your profile?

As you become more experienced your strategy should change

Once you have established an expert witness career you can begin to promote your experience. Keep a record of interesting cases and see if you can make some promotional value from them. Would they make interesting submissions for legal or professional journals?

Can you apply your new skills to other lines of work?

And then think about the qualities you now possess and the new professional contacts you have made. Can you exploit them further? Would other sorts of consultancy work use the same skill sets?

Now let's take a closer look at each approach and consider their advantages and disadvantages.

4.1 Professional bodies

Does your professional body have an expert witness section?

Some professional organisations, like the Royal College of Nursing, the British Medical Association and the Royal Institution of Chartered Surveyors, have set up their own **expert witness sections**. They can offer experts useful advice and support from colleagues within their own profession, and provide enquiring lawyers with search systems to locate suitable experts for cases.

So take a look at the membership bodies to which you belong and give each of them a call. Make enquiries about the sorts of services they could offer you as an expert witness, and whether an additional charge applies.

Advantages

- In general, this service will be free of charge to members. If the organisation does not hold such a list at present, why not ask it to start one?

Disadvantages

- You are reliant on lawyers contacting your professional body to find expert witnesses. How often does this happen? Are the telephones fully manned with knowledgeable staff? Ask them!

You may also like to consider looking around at other relevant membership bodies to which you do not currently belong to see if they offer potentially useful promotional or advice services.

Search for other relevant support organisations too

4.2 Word-of-mouth recommendations

Word-of-mouth recommendation is very powerful

Do not underestimate the power that a **word-of-mouth recommendation** carries. Find out if there are other expert witnesses operating in your locality to see if you can establish some form of 'network'. And tell your work colleagues, friends and acquaintances that you are available for expert witness work. Ensure they all have clear information about where to find your promotional website or marketing material so that they can pass it on to prospective clients.

Ask for written references from lawyers

Once you have received an instruction and completed a case satisfactorily, try to encourage the lawyer to provide a written reference recommending your service to solicitors generally. Ask if you can copy it to prospective instructing lawyers, if appropriate.

A word of warning, though. Lawyers tend to guard their best experts from poaching by other firms. So they will not necessarily be the best source of word-of-mouth recommendations!

Advantages

Let your colleagues know you are taking on expert witness work

- A word-of-mouth recommendation to a lawyer from a professional colleague is worth its weight in gold. Dust off your list of professional and personal contacts and let everyone know you're now taking on expert witness work.

Disadvantages

- You are reliant in part on your professional colleagues forwarding your details. Will they see you as a direct competitor?
- You are also reliant on the good opinion (or otherwise) the prospective instructing lawyer has of the individual making the recommendation. Will he value the recommendation as coming from a reliable source worthy of consideration?

4.3 Local law societies

Find out what your local law society is doing

To date, there are around 120 autonomous local law societies in England and Wales offering a range of services and support to solicitors within their region. They are all supported by regional offices of the Law Society. Some branches hold lists of experts to which you may be able to add your name; others may be willing to provide details of local law firms dealing primarily with litigation.

To obtain the telephone number and contact name for your local branch, simply call the Law Society on 020 7242 1222 and ask for the Communications Department. Alternatively, details of regional branches are available on-line from the Law Society website at www.lawsociety.org.uk.

Experts in Northern Ireland could try registering with the Law Society of Northern Ireland (www.lawsoc-ni.org/), which operates an effective internal expert referral system from its library (call 028 9023 1614). In addition, the Law Society's website provides links to lists of local solicitor associations and solicitor groups.

The Law Society of Scotland does not currently offer a formalised expert referral system. However, its website (www.lawscot.org.uk) does offer links to societies and bar associations within Scotland.

Advantages

- A friendly local law society could be your way into the expert witness scene in your area. You may be able to negotiate free advertising in return for giving a seminar. Or perhaps you could contribute to a regular newsletter, or offer an exclusive time-limited discount for a first instruction from the member firms. Think creatively!

Use your local law society to ease your way into the local law scene

Disadvantages

- You will need to spend some time talking with your local law society official to determine if there are any opportunities worth exploring. Do you have the time or inclination?

It's always a good idea to try to meet lawyers – and, indeed, other expert witnesses – in a low-pressure environment or socially. Time spent chatting over coffee breaks or lunch will give you valuable insights into the problems associated with expert witness work from all sides. And these conversations will also trigger thoughts about how you can improve or adapt your service to better meet the requirements of the lawyer. The key is to build solid respectful relationships with lawyers (and fellow expert witnesses) outside of work that will reap dividends when an instruction is being considered.

Meeting lawyers in a less formal setting is a great way to build your business network

4.4 Local and national media

Establishing regular contact with producers of **local and national radio and television output**, as well as journalists of **local and national newspapers**, is a bit of a double-edged sword. As you will have seen, an ill-placed comment can be publicly embarrassing and lead to ongoing ridicule. However, if you can get it right, you will raise your public profile enormously. It will both:

Fostering links with the media can be a double-edged sword

- increase the possibility of a lawyer contacting you as a result of experiencing your opinion in one media form or another, and
- provide you with more impressive information to add to your CV.

If you are comfortable exploring this option, you will need to:

- **locate media contacts** by searching on-line, reviewing the credits of relevant TV and radio programmes and browsing local and national newspapers
- **explain what you can do** for them

Usually your payment will be the market exposure you receive

- **provide an indication of costs** you would charge (e.g. no charge, travel only, etc.)
- **demonstrate your skills** as, for example, an interviewee, perhaps through an on-line audio or video clip, and
- **offer a sure-fire way of contacting you** 365 days a year at a moment's notice.

Watch out for topical news items that fit with your expertise

Sometimes a 'phone in' radio programme (e.g. BBC Radios 2's lunchtime Jeremy Vine Show) or 'magazine'-style show on television (e.g. BBC Watchdog) can provide an ideal starting point, particularly if your expertise is related to something that is currently newsworthy.

Advantages

- Exposure on TV and radio and in the newspapers will raise your public profile. Ensure your efforts target appropriate media vehicles.

Invest time and money honing your presentation skills – you can't afford a poor interview

Disadvantages

- You'll need to spend time refining your 'broadcast image' and conversational abilities under the pressure of live broadcasts and cameras. Are you comfortable under such pressure?

- Public media exposure can backfire if you say something without thinking. Is it worth the risk? Should you wait until you have a few years of expert witness work under your belt?
- You'll need to contact TV, radio and newspaper editors. Do you have the time?
- You should also consider creating an appropriate marketing piece on-line, including a video/audio clip. Can you do this yourself, or would you need to buy in the skills?

Start local to 'test the water'

Remember to start slowly, refining your media skills on local projects. It's more cost-effective to make a handful of well-placed calls and follow each up until you are able to speak directly to the relevant journalist. Then monitor the news and ensure you are proactive if an appropriate story comes to light.

4.5 Professional journals, newsletters, etc.

Play to your strengths: only write articles if you are a really good written communicator

If you are particularly good with the pen, try writing articles for publication in legal and professional journals and newsletters. This is a time-consuming opportunity, but a well-placed entertaining article on a popular or newsworthy topic will produce results.

You could consider:

- diarising a day in the life of an expert witness
- reporting on a particularly interesting case in which you have been involved (ensuring you have permission to do so and employing suitable anonymisation)
- commenting on a newsworthy topic of relevance to your discipline or expert witness work in general

- advising lawyers about how to analyse reports in your discipline and the questions they should be asking themselves
- offering advice about choosing a reliable expert witness in your discipline.

Publishing articles on your expert witness activities can round-out your CV

Of course, you can record the publication of all articles in your CV or résumé to underline your knowledge of expert witness practice and how well your opinion is received by others.

Advantages

- If you already possess the writing skills and have sufficient time to keep abreast of the news, then the only cost to you is your time.

Disadvantages

- If writing is not your forte, efforts made here may well be time wasted. Would it be better to spend time exploring other avenues?
- You could choose to employ a publicity writer to respond to any media enquiries. Can you afford this luxury?
- Do you have the time to locate the journals, maintain contact with them, and proactively seek to write relevant articles?

Some legal journals publish expert witness material

There are a number of national legal journals and newsletters, some of which publish expert witness supplements. The main contacts are listed below.

- **The Law Society Gazette**
  www.lawgazette.co.uk
  Tel 020 7841 5541
- **The Lawyer**
  www.thelawyer.com
  Tel 020 7943 8102

- **New Law Journal**
  www.new-law-journal.co.uk
  Tel 020 7400 2500
- **Solicitors Journal**
  www.solicitorsjournal.com
  Tel 020 7490 0049
- **The Legal Executive**
  www.ilex.org.uk
  Tel 01234 845713
- **The Scots Law Times**
  www.wgreen.co.uk/scotslaw
  Tel 0131 225 4879
- **Journal of the Law Society of Scotland**
  www.journalonline.co.uk
  Tel 0131 561 0021
- **The Writ**
  www.lawsoc-ni.org/writ/ind99.htm
  Tel 028 9042 8899

Search on-line for specialist publications and organisations involving lawyers in relevant disciplines and ask whether they offer additional more targeted promotional opportunities. For example:

Use the internet to research more targeted promotional opportunities

- **Criminal Law Week** (a weekly digest of developments in the criminal law)
  www.criminal-law.co.uk
- **Independent Lawyer** (for legal aid solicitors and barristers)
  www.independent-lawyer.com
- **Society for Computers & Law Journal**
  www.scl.org
- **Association of Personal Injury Lawyers**
  www.apil.org.uk

4.6 Talks and presentations

Contribute to, or organise, meetings of potential clients

If you have the time and inclination, consider organising talks or presentations that offer you access to potential clients, e.g. solicitors, legal executives, etc. A visible presence at gatherings of potential clients will help to build your reputation and enhance your CV.

You could also consider getting involved in expert witness conferences and seminars. They are ideal networking opportunities. A number are held throughout the year by the following expert witness bodies:

- **Academy of Experts**
  www.academy-experts.org
  Tel 020 7430 0333
- **Expert Witness Institute**
  www.ewi.org.uk
  Tel 0870 366 6367
- **Society of Expert Witnesses**
  www.sew.org.uk
  Tel 0845 702 3014
- **Bond Solon** Annual Expert Witness Conference
  www.bondsolon.com
  Tel 020 7253 7053

Advantages

An interesting, engaging talk will boost your reputation

- An impressive talk to an audience of experts or lawyers, together with the associated networking opportunities, has the potential to build your business contacts and increase your flow of instructions.

Disadvantages

- You will need to spend time locating possible 'vehicles' for your presentation and then approach the organiser to see if you can get involved.
- You will need to spend time preparing an appropriate presentation for each audience.
- Obviously, a poor performance will generate no work and could even be damaging to your current reputation.

A poorly delivered talk will damage your reputation

- How well you deal with follow up questions will be scrutinised closely.

4.7 Expert witness directories

One of the easiest ways of promoting yourself as an expert witness is to register with one of the expert witness directories. Registration is simple, with some offering vetting for added value. Supply your details and a credit card payment and your searchable details could be on-line within 24 hours.

A directory entry is a quick and easy way to advertise your availability

A word of warning, though. It's easy to get confused between the directories because, for obvious reasons, they all have similar sounding titles. Ensure you know which you are talking to, otherwise you may end up joining a directory you had previously discounted.

CAUTION: Be clear which directory you are dealing with

Advantages

- The expert witness directories are relatively easy to find by searching on-line. Each has its own **distribution method**, saving you the costs associated with direct mail efforts.

Take time to determine the benefits of each directory listing

- The directories usually **typeset your details**, removing the need for you to arrange your own advert.

- Most lawyers are aware that such directories exist and may use their on-line services without prompting.
- The directory publishers **maintain their own lawyer databases**, saving you time and money.
- Publishers make your details available in a variety of formats, including **in print, on-line and on CD-ROM**.
- Directories can attract work from **across the UK**, if not **worldwide**.

A vetted directory adds kudos

- Some directories undertake **vetting** of expert witnesses for quality control purposes. Vetted experts often refer to their entries in reputable directories in their CVs, and can also use **logos** provided by the directories.

Look at added value too

- Some directories offer inclusive **helplines** and **newsletters**, adding value to the cost of an entry.

Disadvantages

Perform a value-for-money comparison

- The costs of directory entries vary enormously between publishers. Compare product quality and format, distribution methods and associated services to select best value for money.

Don't rely on lawyers to know which directory they found you in!

- You are reliant on the publisher to distribute your details. And you can only assess effectiveness when questioning a new lawyer contact. Be aware that lawyers also confuse these directories. So always check carefully where an instruction has come from.
- Your details are contained within a database of your competitors, rather than you seeming to be the only expert available for this sort of work.

The **most popular vetted directories** publish in print and on-line, offering these formats to improve market penetration. They are:

Two vetted directories lead the way

- **The UK Register of Expert Witnesses**
  (vetting available)
  On-line, on CD-ROM, printed book
  Publisher: J S Publications, Newmarket
  First published 1988
  www.jspubs.com
  Tel 01638 561590
- **Expert Witness Directory**
  (vetting available)
  On-line, printed book
  Publisher: Sweet & Maxwell, London
  First published 1996
  www.legalhub.co.uk
  Tel 020 7393 7000

There are also several internet-only searchable databases which can be found using on-line search engines. Ensure you check their standing in the marketplace before parting with money.

On-line only directories exist, but be clear about their reputation and currency

And just to be absolutely clear, **always be certain who you are dealing with** when speaking to the directories.

4.8 Agencies

Expert reporting organisations, usually medical (MROs), exist to manage the provision of expert reports for solicitors and insurers. Typically, an agency offers solicitors an inclusive package of services that encompasses:

MROs make their money by sitting between the lawyer and the expert

- finding an expert
- obtaining relevant records
- issuing instructions

- setting up an examination
- chasing the report, and
- paying the expert.

MROs complicate debt recovery when things go wrong

However, the **financial instability** and **lack of industry regulation** associated with such organisations have made many experts wary of involvement. But for lawyers and insurers, they offer an easy way to obtain reports quickly from across the UK, even though costs are inflated by the involvement of the middlemen.

Pay close attention to the credit you extend to MROs

So, if you want to sign up to a contract with such an organisation, read the wording very carefully, ensure you minimise your financial exposure to them and chase payment promptly and doggedly.

Advantages

- You can **leave the task of finding work completely to others** – although that can also be seen as a dangerously narrow marketing strategy.
- So long as the agency is profitable (and several have gone bankrupt over the past few years), you **may get paid sooner** than if you were instructed directly.

Disadvantages

MROs can create more problems than they solve

- There's **no guarantee of work**, and leaving the job to someone else may only delay the time when you'll need to take hold of the task yourself.
- **If the agency goes bust (and several have recently), you are very likely to end up with no payment of your fees**. A direct contractual relationship with a law firm will offer a generally better payment record and a far better quality of instruction.

- Using a 'middleman' can **get in the way of forming a good working relationship with your instructing lawyer**. Indeed, when working through an MRO you can be wholly unaware of the name of your instructing lawyer or his firm.

MROs hamper the professional relationship between expert and lawyer

- Instructions via agencies are **unlikely to lead to repeat instructions** from a lawyer.
- You may well need to make an **upfront payment** of several hundred pounds to register with the agency. Check to see if the agency guarantees work.
- You will probably need to **agree to charge the agency at a set hourly rate or rate per report**.
- The **agency will add a percentage to your fee** and charge the lawyer itself. By working direct with the lawyer, you can charge more for your services while still charging less than an MRO.

4.9 Legal press adverts

All legal publications have space allocated for display advertising. The task for you is to assess the target markets of each journal and decide which, if any, are worth using as an advertising vehicle. Occasionally publishers run expert witness supplements or special features, so be sure to keep in touch with them so you know when the special issues are due.

Display adverts in legal magazines are relatively expensive

Advantages

- There are many magazines and journals that target legal minds. Some are national, while others are local. Some specialise in particular areas of law or target particular groups of lawyer. They are easy to locate and contact for advertising schedules and rates by searching the internet. See §4.5 for some contact details.

A wide range of publications exist, from national to specialist

- The journals and magazines maintain their own databases of contacts. Do check their distribution figures, though. You will also save on all the costs associated with a direct mail.

Disadvantages

Repeat adverts work better than one-off placements

- You will have to accept that advertising like this will require significant up-front funding and may or may not lead to enquiries. Agreeing to repeat adverts over several issues will generally attract discounts and may improve response rates.
- You will need to design an impressive-looking advert that sets you apart from the crowd, output the file at the correct resolution and format, and then send it to the publisher. Can you do this yourself, or will you need to buy in the expertise?

Ensure the readership is your target market

- You will not know who is receiving the magazine/journal or viewing your advert. Many lawyer readers will not be litigators, unless you choose a magazine specifically for litigators. The only way you'll know if the advert is working is if someone contacts you as a result – and if you remember to ask them how they got your details!

Expert witness directories are much more targeted

- Advertising in this way is generally more expensive than through expert witness directories. Furthermore, anyone consulting an expert witness directory is going to be looking for an expert witness, so there is much less wastage.

4.10 Mailshots

Use direct mail to get yourself onto internal lists of experts held by law firms

Many law firms keep internal lists of experts, so a mailshot including your CV and a résumé of your experience as an expert witness may be filed for future reference.

You'll need to create the following:

- quality **promotional material** (which need not be expensive)
- a **tailored CV**
- an indication of your **fee scales**, and
- a **well-written covering letter** ideally addressed to an individual within a firm.

A copy of your current **terms and conditions** may also prove useful, but is not essential.

Mailshot databases can be either created by you or purchased from specialist database suppliers.

Advantages

- You can target local law firms or firms that specialise in cases relevant to your expertise.
- If you can get your information into the hands of an interested litigator, he **may** file it for future use.

Disadvantages

- Direct mail is *not* a cheap option. You have to buy or locate and input the databases, create and print the mailing items (brochures, letters, envelopes, etc.), stuff the mailshot and then pay for postage.

Large-scale direct mail is not a cheap option

- The vast majority of direct mail items do not reach an interested party. A response rate of 2% is considered good! Repeat mailings (changing the letter and advertising materials) as part of a marketing campaign are necessary to begin to penetrate the market.

Plan a campaign of mailings and monitor response diligently

4.10.1 Self-created databases

For building your own database, a useful starting point is *Waterlow's Solicitors' & Barristers' Directory* (www.waterlow.com) or the *Law Society's Directory of Solicitors and Barristers* (www.lawsociety.org.

Building your own list from public sources is time-consuming

uk and click on 'Find a solicitor'). Copies should be available for consultation at most central libraries and the databases can be accessed on-line.

Scottish solicitors are listed on-line through the Law Society of Scotland's website at www.lawscot.org.uk, while solicitors in Northern Ireland are listed on the Law Society of Northern Ireland's website at www. lawsoc-ni.org.

There are many other on-line websites available for interrogation, including www.lawyerlocator.co.uk.

Once built, you'll need to maintain your databases

Remember to:

- ensure that you **comply with the Data Protection Act** 1998
- regularly **check your databases** to ensure that repeat mailshots are still being sent to the right person at the right address.

4.10.2 Database sales

Commercially available lists can save you lots of time

The following companies sell tailored databases for mailshot use:

- **J S Publications** sells to experts, under the name of **LawyerLists**, subsets of its main solicitor mailing list to experts as either labels or a database for multiple use. For an additional charge letterhead can be overprinted. Surf to www.jspubs.com/lawyerlist for more detailed information.
- **Records Department of the Law Society of England and Wales** – for a fee it will provide details of solicitors in a given locality. www.lawsociety.org.uk
- **Waterlow Direct Marketing** – commercial database seller – www.wdmlists.com/legal/

4.10.3 Shared mailshots

Shared mailings can be cost-effective

Alternatively, why not consider a targeted **'shared' mailshot**? There are a number of companies offering conferences and courses to the legal profession. For a fee, they will include promotional material from a third party in their mailshots. For example, CLT (www.clt.co.uk) can target firms of solicitors by specialism, geographic region and size. For further details, call CLT on 0121 355 0900. You might also consider arranging to have your details included in delegate packs for conferences and courses. However, do check that the profile of delegates matches your target market.

Advantages

- If you are going to go to the expense of creating promotional material, postal costs can be saved by joining together with other experts or other legal service providers in shared mailings.

Disadvantages

- Your promotional material becomes one of many and may lose its impact. Is the cost saving worth this loss?
- You will need to locate shared mailing opportunities, which will take some time.

4.11 Legal conferences

Exhibition space is costly for the small business

Another way of reaching legal professionals is through exhibitions and conferences at which stands are available for hire. Such an approach can be quite costly. Therefore you would be well advised to perform an accurate cost:benefit analysis prior to committing yourself.

Relevant professional bodies should be able to provide information on key events. They may also be in a position to offer advice on how to get listed as a potential speaker – an ideal way of promoting your own expert witness services or trading exhibition space for a presentation!

The contacts listed below are just some of those that offer experts the opportunity to rent either a stand or space at some of their events. There are many others; internet searching will provide the answers.

- **Law Society of England and Wales**
  www.lawsociety.org.uk
- **The Bar Council**
  www.barcouncil.org.uk
- **Law Society of Scotland**
  www.lawscot.org.uk
- **Law Society of Northern Ireland**
  www.lawsoc-ni.org
- **Association of Personal Injury Lawyers**
  www.apil.org.uk

Advantages

- You will have the potential to meet many lawyers. But do you have the right personality to attract the crowds?
- If you can trade exhibition space for a presentation to enhance the conference programme, then it may be worth attending.
- If you can locate a small specialist conference that will not attract the big corporations, you may find that rates for stands are more affordable.

Disadvantages

- Exhibition space at large legal conferences is hugely expensive. You will be competing with global corporations with enormous marketing budgets, multiple staff and large glossy display areas. For most experts, the costs far outweigh the benefits.

- Many lawyers view exhibitors as people to be avoided on the way to the coffee area. How is the conference set up? Will lawyers have time to visit you? Will you proactively try to attract visitors, or will you sit meekly in a corner?

Unless you are proactive, you will be wasting your time and money

4.12 Growing your business with ADR

One option to consider when seeking to expand your expert business is the various forms of alternative dispute resolution (ADR). ADR offers alternatives to litigation that can be used to settle a claim. Forms of ADR include:

ADR can sit well alongside an expert witness practice

- **arbitration**
- **early neutral evaluation** (ENE)
- **conciliation**
- **mediation**
- **adjudication**, and
- **expert determination**.

Each requires a keen analytical mind and good communication and people management skills. Below are outlined each of the more common forms of ADR that may be of interest when you wish to diversify.

4.12.1 Arbitration

Arbitration is an adjudication process, normally held **in private**, operating outside the court system. A third party (one arbitrator or a panel of arbitrators) is asked to reach a decision that is **binding** on all the parties involved. Arbitration hearings may well be **less formal** than court hearings, and the

Arbitration hands over decision-making control to a third party

exact procedure will be decided in advance by the arbitrator.

The arbitrator's decision is binding on all the parties

While arbitration proceedings may be **less expensive** and **more accessible** than litigation, the arbitration process differs from mediation by giving over to a third party complete control for the decision making.

An arbitrator can be a lawyer or any professional who is an expert in the contested field and who understands the nature of the issues in dispute. He will be independent of all the parties.

Expert witnesses, professional witnesses and witnesses of fact can be called to give evidence at arbitration hearings.

4.12.2 Early neutral evaluation

ENE offers a frank, confidential evaluation of the legal merits of a dispute

Early neutral evaluation (ENE) is an effective way of facilitating an out-of-court settlement of a high-value case prior to a formal judicial ruling. Costs are usually split equally between the parties.

Anyone can conduct the ENE, but it is usually a judge or someone who is legally qualified.

An ENE will provide parties to a dispute with an early and frank confidential evaluation of the legal merits of the dispute. The ENE 'judge' will:

- **study all materials** provided in advance of the ENE
- **perform independent research** into relevant case law as necessary
- **consider presentations** carefully (written and/or oral)
- **clarify positions and facts** through questioning, and

- **prepare a carefully worded but direct evaluation**.

Unlike mediation, ENE focuses specifically on the key issues raised by the facts of a case and the relevant law. However, it need not be confined to the arguments raised by the parties. An ENE 'judge' reviews all of the available evidence and gauges what is likely to happen at a trial. The ruling is **without prejudice** and is **non-binding**.

ENE is without prejudice and non-binding

4.12.3 Conciliation

Parties to a dispute come to a conciliator to seek guidance. A skilled conciliator will assist the parties by driving their negotiations and directing them towards a satisfactory agreement. Conciliation is a much **less adversarial** process than arbitration.

A skilled conciliator makes proposals for settlement

Key features of a conciliator include:

- The conciliator plays a relatively **direct role** in the resolution of a dispute.
- The conciliator **advises the parties** on certain solutions by making proposals for settlement.
- The conciliator is usually seen as an **authority figure** who is responsible for determining the best solution for the parties.
- The conciliator, not the parties, often **develops and proposes the terms of settlement**.

Ultimately, it is **the parties to the dispute who make decisions about the proposals made** by the conciliator. This makes the role of a conciliator distinct from the role of a mediator.

A conciliator helps the parties to agree on a way forward

4.12.4 Mediation

Mediation is the most popular and widely recognised form of ADR in the UK. It employs negotiation

Mediation is the most common form of ADR in the UK

techniques to their fullest and offers solutions beyond those a court could ordinarily impose.

Mediation is a structured process, whereby two or more parties to a dispute attempt by themselves, on a voluntary basis, to reach an agreement on settlement with the assistance of a mediator. This process may be initiated by the parties or suggested or ordered by a court. It includes mediation conducted by a judge who is not responsible for any judicial proceedings concerning the dispute in question.

A mediator helps the parties to find a mutually agreeable solution

A mediator is specially trained to assist parties in settling disputes. He acts as an impartial neutral catalyst who helps the parties to arrive at a mutually agreed solution. The mediator has **no power to impose a settlement** on either party.

Where direct negotiation has failed and the parties are in deadlock, mediation offers the opportunity for the parties to move forward with the professional assistance of a mediator.

In the lifecycle of a dispute, mediation can be useful at almost any stage. Unlike court proceedings, mediation involves the direct participation of the parties, who often work alongside instructed legal representatives on a proactive and creative basis.

A mediator is a facilitator and does not determine any issues

The role and function of the mediator is not to determine the issues but to assist the parties in:

- **identifying issues and information needs**
- **reducing obstacles** to communication
- **exploring alternatives**, and
- **focusing on the needs and interests of those most affected** by the dispute.

Mediation seeks common ground between the parties

The objective of the mediation process is to help the parties visualise alternative solutions. The mediator is tasked with guiding the parties to areas of common ground.

Some cases are inherently not suited to settlement, and in these instances the determinative process of a court decision is the only alternative. Should mediation fail, the process is not wasted because it serves as a useful way of information gathering and formulating the underlying case in dispute.

4.12.5 Adjudication

Adjudication is the legal process by which an arbiter or judge reviews evidence and arguments, including legal reasoning set out by opposing parties or litigants, to come to a decision which **determines rights and obligations between the parties** involved. Three types of dispute are resolved through adjudication:

Adjudication involves a determination of rights and obligations

- disputes between private parties, such as individuals or corporations
- disputes between private parties and public officials, and
- disputes between public officials or public bodies.

The most common application is in the construction and engineering industries in resolving construction contract disputes. The majority of disputes are resolved quickly in an informal environment by dialogue and negotiation, enabling construction and engineering works to continue undisrupted.

Adjudication is most common in the construction and engineering fields

4.12.6 Expert determination

Expert determination is a **confidential** and **binding** process that can offer an effective means of settling a technical issue or dispute. It is particularly appropriate for technical or valuation disputes. The

Expert determination is confidential and binding

process offers the parties an **informal** and **flexible** environment suitable for settlement.

Any agreed person can perform the expert determination

Determination of the dispute is by an independent person with expertise relevant to the dispute. Anyone who has been agreed by the parties to be an expert in the relevant field can perform the expert determination. Often, the identity of the independent expert will have been agreed prior to the dispute arising.

The expert can adopt procedures suited to the particular circumstances of the case. During the process, the expert must act fairly and each party must be given a reasonable opportunity to be heard and respond to the other party.

Expert determination is quick and relatively inexpensive

When a fast solution is needed, expert determination is often the **quickest** and **most inexpensive** way of resolving disputes (particularly when the facts are agreed). And in a commercially sensitive case, the expert determination can be carried out **in private**, thus guaranteeing protection of confidences.

Expert determination has the following advantages compared with other methods of ADR:

- It allows the **appointment of an expert who is familiar with the technical issues** in dispute.
- It is usually **cheaper, quicker and less formal** than other methods.
- It **helps parties to maintain business relationships** (it is confidential and less adversarial than litigation or arbitration).

Expert determination can preserve working business relationships

The expert's decision is normally final and **binding**, unless the parties challenge it on grounds of, for example, fraud or partiality.

In England and Wales, the result of an expert determination can be enforced through the courts.

However, this may not be the case in other jurisdictions. For that reason, international disputes may be better resolved using another form of ADR.

Parties will have to pay for the costs of the expert and will normally bear their own costs. There is usually no power for the expert to award costs in favour of the successful party.

4.12.7 Useful addresses

- Academy of Experts, 3 Gray's Inn Square, London, WC1R 5AH (Tel 020 7430 0333) www.academy-experts.org
- The Centre for Effective Dispute Resolution (CEDR), International Dispute Resolution Centre, 70 Fleet Street, London, EC4Y 1EU (Tel 020 7536 6000) www.cedr.co.uk.
- UK College of Family Mediators, Alexander House, Telephone Avenue, Bristol, BS1 4BS (Tel 0117 904 7223) www.ukcfm.co.uk
- Chartered Institute of Arbitrators, International Arbitration & Mediation Centre, 12 Bloomsbury Square, London, WC1A 2LP (Tel 020 7421 7444) www.arbitrators.org
- ADR Group, Grove House, Grove Road, Redland, Bristol, BS6 6UN (Tel 0117 946 7180) www.adrgroup.co.uk
- UK Mediation Ltd, 8 Green Lane, Belper, Derbyshire, DE56 1BY (Tel 01773 822222) www.ukmediation.net
- National Mediation Helpline, Clerks Room, Equity House, Blackbrook Park Avenue, Taunton, TA1 2PX (Tel 0845 603 0809) www.nationalmediationhelpline.com

- The Adjudication Society, c/o Fenwick Elliott LLP, Aldwych House, 71-91 Aldwych, London, WC2B 4HN (Tel 01865 310702) www.adjudication.org
- Advisory, Conciliation and Arbitration Service (ACAS), The Cube, 123 Albion Street, Leeds, LS2 8ER (Tel 08457 474747) www.acas.org.uk

4.13 Expert witness marketing summary

Create direct contacts with lawyers

- You should aim to **maximise direct contacts with lawyers**. Quite apart from making payment easier, valuable professional relationships will be developed that will follow the lawyer wherever he moves. Furthermore, knowing that your instructing lawyer is just a telephone call or e-mail away for advice or clarification can be a comforting thought.

Achieve a diverse range of clients

- It's easy to accept repeat instructions from a regular lawyer or law firm client. However, effort must be put in to **diversifying your client base**. If a law firm merges or closes, you do not want to be left having lost a large part of your workload. By conducting research on an ongoing basis you should be well placed to identify new instructing solicitors and law firms and thus update your network of contacts.
- **Investigate your competitors** and gather information about how they promote their services. Use the results to inform your marketing strategy.

Keep your promotional material current

- Ensure you **keep your website, promotional material and CV up to date**. Revisit both at least every 3 months and refine the text, images, etc., in line with your career and service developments.

Always monitor the effectiveness of your marketing

- In any form of marketing it is vital to **monitor response** so that you can better target your advertising budget the following year. But be aware of possible confusion arising from sources with similar sounding names. Make a point of always asking instructing solicitors *exactly* how and from where they obtained your details.

- Remember that **first impressions** really do count. Ensure that your professionalism is not jeopardised by the manner in which your telephone is answered or a message is taken. (This is particularly relevant when your contact number is your domestic residence rather than a business number.) At all times your dress and manner should reflect the degree of professionalism and gravitas commensurate with the role of an expert witness.

Always give the right impression to your clients

- Have your updated **CV readily accessible** on-line (ideally) or through the post. Make it as easy as possible for lawyers to find out more about you without having to speak with you. Think about what they will want to know (e.g. fees, turnaround time, flexibility for court appearances, familiarity with SJE work, credit terms, etc.), and provide them with the answers.

Keep your CV current and accurate

- And finally, make time to **revisit your marketing strategy on a regular basis**. It will need to change to reflect your business development plan and your own life–work balance requirements.

Marketing is a process, not an end in itself

5

Deskwork

Most instructions follow a similar path

The deskwork associated with a case will vary little, regardless of whether the case is civil, criminal or family. All types of proceeding require expert witnesses:

- to **act according to similar rules of court and procedure**
- to **write well-structured reports**, based on clear and thorough thinking
- if required, to **answer questions of clarification** on their reports, and
- if required, to **take part in expert discussions** before the hearing to try to identify areas of agreement and narrow down areas of disagreement.

Always apply standard rules of business

As an expert witness, in all cases you should adhere to what should be considered standard rules of business.

- You **must not be biased** towards your instructing party. You should **remain wholly independent** at all times.
- You should **record accurately the time spent** on each case so that billing can be transparent, unambiguous and justifiable.
- You should **respond promptly to all enquiries** from instructing parties.
- You should **ensure those instructing you are kept informed** of progress.
- You must **ensure that your written contract is in place**, properly signed, before work commences on a case.
- You must **ensure the security of any important documents** in your care.

- You should **ensure that professional indemnity insurance is in place** and covers your expert witness work.
- You **must not disclose privileged documents**.
- You **must consult your instructing party if you are at all uncertain** of your instructions.
- You **must stay within your area of expertise**. Whilst it is recognised that the boundary of your competence will rarely be sharply defined, you should be clear at all times when you are being taken away from your core competency.

This chapter takes you through a typical instruction, focusing on the expected deskwork in a case. It will consider:

- receiving an **initial enquiry**
- receiving and acknowledging **instructions**
- writing your draft and final **reports**, and
- answering **written questions**.

Always know the rules that govern the instruction

The various rules, practice directions and protocols for civil, criminal and family proceedings offer some guidance to experts and lawyers on procedure. See the appendices for full details.

What follows draws its focus from civil procedures, but the criminal and family procedures are similar. Any important differences are noted in the text.

5.1 Initial enquiry

An initial enquiry is often quite informal

Let us assume that a solicitor has located a suitable expert, and that's you! He will need to contact you direct to:

- **outline the matter** on which assistance is required

- **confirm the appropriateness of your expertise** by exploring how your experience and qualifications mesh with the issues in the case
- **establish your availability and resources** for undertaking the assignment, and
- **check that there are no potential conflicts of interest**.

All this can be done by letter, of course, but it is more likely that an initial enquiry of this kind will be made by telephone.

Determine at the outset how the case is funded

The solicitor may go on to ask you for a **CV** confirming your experience, academic qualifications and professional training appropriate to the assignment. At this point, too, the solicitor ought to make clear how the litigation is being funded, e.g. LSC, private client, etc. It is important to ascertain the funding mechanism early on so that you can:

The funding mechanism will inform your view on credit control

- **control your credit exposure**
- **manage your solicitor** (e.g. check that prior authority has been received), and
- **inform your fee chasing** decisions.

5.2 Expert response

Be quick to refuse an instruction you can't take on

There are various ways in which you can respond to a solicitor's initial enquiry. It might be, of course, that you lack the appropriate expertise, are simply not available to carry out the assignment outlined, or are not interested in undertaking it. If that is the case, you should say so immediately.

Assuming, though, that you are both available and interested, the initial response to the enquiry could prove crucial to a satisfactory outcome.

5.2.1 Contracts

If you have worked for the solicitor before and on that previous occasion the solicitor behaved impeccably, there may be no harm in expressing there and then a willingness to assist again – subject, that is, to your usual terms of engagement. Even so, it is always wise to follow up any verbal expression of willingness with a letter to both confirm this and either incorporating your terms or attaching a copy of them.

Always use a written set of terms

It is absolutely **essential** that you adopt this procedure if:

- it is the first time you have been approached by anyone from the law firm, or
- you are less than happy with the way in which you were treated previously by the firm.

Remember that in no sense does 'willingness to assist' imply a commitment to do so – that comes only after:

There's no commitment until the formalities have been completed

- your **terms have been agreed**
- you have been **fully instructed**, and
- you have **accepted the instructions**.

Terms of engagement are dealt with more fully in another book in this series (Little Book 1: *Expert Witness Fees*), but it is pertinent to repeat the warning given there about the weasel words some solicitors use when asked to confirm their acceptance of terms. They may, for example, 'acknowledge receipt' of your terms or state that they 'understand' them. Both expressions fall a long way short of what is needed.

Beware weasel words designed to avoid agreement of your terms!

To obviate the risk of wily solicitors devising statements of 'acceptance' along these lines, you may prefer to enclose with your terms of

Get your terms signed and returned

engagement a printed form for the solicitor to sign and return which confirms acceptance in words of your choosing.

5.2.2 Type of advice

Always be clear about the type of work required

At this stage, too, you should seek to establish the kind of assistance the solicitor requires, i.e. whether it is private advice or the preparation of evidence for use in court – if not already apparent. Ultimately, of course, your help may be sought for both purposes. But it is as well for them to be clearly distinguished from the outset. While instructions for advice are privileged against disclosure, those requiring the preparation of evidence are not.

5.2.3 Fees

Who is the paymaster?

If the solicitor has not already volunteered the information, you should enquire how and by whom your fees and expenses are to be paid.

If the solicitor needs your expert advice to decide whether to take on a case, then the cost of obtaining it is a business overhead of the law firm and it alone would be responsible for paying your bill.

If prior authority is needed, ask for confirmation that it has been obtained

In other circumstances the solicitor may need to obtain prior authority to engage your services. If this prior authority is lacking, the relevant party might refuse to reimburse the solicitor for the charges you make. That could be the beginning of a long drawn-out battle to get paid. You would be well advised to ensure prior authority has been obtained before commencing any work.

5.3 Initial briefing

In simple cases, instructions are usually by letter or telephone

Lawyers will generally seek to minimise the expense of instructing experts where possible. So in straightforward cases lawyers will frequently choose to brief you by letter or telephone. If the matter is at all complex, though, instruction may have to be done face to face.

Either way, the lawyer needs to explain the dispute in sufficient depth for you to understand the issues to be addressed. It is, after all, much easier to frame the answer to a question if you understand the context in which it is being asked!

Lawyers must give clear instructions, so query any ambiguity or uncertainty

An initial briefing of this kind should establish for you those matters the solicitor regards as relevant to the outcome of the case. It should also give you the opportunity to make clear any aspect of the assignment:

- with which you may be **unfamiliar**,
- which you are **not qualified** to tackle, or
- for which the **assistance of others** might be required.

5.3.1 Estimates

It is at this juncture that the question of cost is most likely to arise. Even if the lawyer does not ask for an estimate, it is always prudent to provide one.

An estimate will help to avoid an unexpectedly large fee

Assuming you charge an hourly rate, the estimate should itemise the time each stage of the assignment is expected to take. By simple multiplication and addition, the total fee likely to be charged by the end of the case should be stated clearly.

Travelling time may be included for the purposes of this calculation. However, the actual expense of air, rail or taxi fares should always be reckoned, and ultimately charged for, at cost, along with any other disbursements you anticipate incurring while carrying out the assignment.

Out-of-pocket disbursements should be charged at cost

There are three other points concerning estimates that are worth bearing in mind.

Keep a detailed record of the time you spend

The first is that if an estimate has been computed on the basis of an hourly rate, you must keep a record of:

- the **amount of time** each day that you spend on the assignment, and
- the **nature of the work** undertaken.

Your timesheet will justify your bill

This worksheet should then be submitted with your invoice. Even though the amount of time it records may be less than that estimated initially, the instructing solicitor could be required to produce it when the court comes to assess the costs of the case.

Estimates are not binding, but be quick to inform the lawyer should costs spiral

Remember that **estimates are never binding**. However, you do need to inform your instructing solicitor if it should ever become apparent that you have underestimated:

- the time it will take to complete a job or
- the expenses you will be incurring along the way.

The solicitor's authority to continue should always be sought.

For lengthy cases staged billing is quite acceptable

Finally, there is no reason why invoices for your work should not be submitted in stages, especially if the case is proceeding to trial. In any event, most experts submit an invoice with their final report, whether or not the case is expected to go further.

5.3.2 Clarity

Poor instructions lead to unfocused reports

It should go without saying that **solicitors ought to provide clear instructions**, but sadly they do not always do so. Sometimes this is through incompetence; more often it stems from slipshod thinking. Whatever the reason, a failure to instruct properly is likely to result in an expert report that is unfocused or inadequate in other ways. As a result, the report may require considerable reworking before it can be submitted to the court or exchanged with the other side – and all at the client's expense.

Beware woolly instructions

You should be particularly wary of instructions that call you to investigate 'any other issues you may consider relevant'. Such phrases open up the possibility of recriminations later on, should you omit to cover an issue that turns out to be crucial to the outcome of the case. This is why you should always insist on having written instructions, or at any rate written confirmation of any instructions given verbally, before work commences. This applies regardless of whether you have met previously with the solicitor to discuss the matter.

Be quick to ask for more detail if needed

You need the opportunity that written instructions afford to reflect on the technical issues the case presents and to let the solicitor know if there is any other information required to carry out the assignment. Likely questions arising will include:

- Are there **witness statements** to be seen, or **reports from experts** who have been instructed to deal with other aspects of the case?
- If proceedings have already been issued, can a copy of the **statement of claim or defence** be provided?
- What of the **other documents** in the case, e.g. medical records?
- Is **permission** needed to visit the site/examine the patient, and, if so, has this been obtained?

'The 3 Cs': instructions should be clear, cogent and complete

The main requirement for instructions is that they should be **specific and unambiguous**. The amount of detail they provide will depend on the type of case and the frequency with which the solicitor has instructed you in the past.

5.3.3 Objectivity

Clients must understand that only an unbiased expert will help their case

Clients often have difficulty coming to terms with the idea that the expert for whom they are paying is not someone who will go into court and argue their position, come what may.

For their part, solicitors need to be sensitive to this. Clients must be convinced that **only unbiased expert evidence will do their case any good**.

It is very important, though, to ensure that you fully understand the need for **objectivity** in your reports and in any evidence given from the witness box.

5.4 Letter of instruction

Written instructions are not privileged, so careful wording is required

A solicitor should take great care in framing the written instructions he gives you, in particular because the **contents of the letter of instruction are not privileged**. Furthermore, it is unlikely to help the client if the court should perceive the instructions to be subjectively slanted. Quite apart from the sanctions the court may impose on that count, there is also the risk that it may refuse to allow the client to rely on any part of your expert report.

5.4.1 Minimum requirements

The solicitor's letter of instruction should at the very least state:

Are you being instructed by one party or jointly by all the parties?

i) **the party** for whom the solicitor is acting and whether the solicitor is seeking to appoint you on behalf of that party alone or jointly with another party to the dispute (in which event you will also need to know when and how to contact that other party)

ii) the sort of **assistance required**, i.e. a report for advice only or one for use in court

iii) the precise kind of **expertise** called for

iv) an **outline history** of the matter, identifying any factual aspects that are in dispute

v) the **assumed facts**, i.e. those you are not required to investigate, often because they are agreed by the other party

You will be given the facts upon which you will form an opinion

vi) the **issues** on which your opinion is being sought

vii) details of **relevant documents** to be supplied by the solicitor on acceptance of instructions, and whether these will need to be returned to the solicitor in due course

viii) **whether proceedings have started**, and, if so, in which court (and to which track the case has been allocated in civil proceedings) and whether the court has issued any directions with regard to expert evidence

ix) any **time constraints** on the provision of advice or the submission of reports – and, if proceedings have started, the date(s) fixed for the hearing

Ensure you have the time to complete the instruction

x) **basic information** such as contact names, addresses and telephone numbers.

It is also desirable for the solicitor to disclose the names of any other experts already instructed in the case.

It is in the interests of all concerned that you should raise at this stage any queries about the instructions received. The solicitor should respond promptly to requests for clarification.

Always seek clarification if necessary

Above all, you should never accept instructions if there is any uncertainty as to whether you will be able to complete the assignment within a reasonable time or according to any timetable the court may have set for the exchange of expert reports.

Ensure you can attend any court hearings

Similarly, you should not accept instructions in a case for which a court appearance will be required if there is any likelihood that you will not be available to give evidence when the case comes to trial.

5.4.2 Role of the expert

In most cases, letters of instruction will go no further than requesting a report. But you should be aware that once the report has been provided it may not be the end of your involvement.

Most civil cases don't reach court

For example, the majority of civil cases are settled before they reach court, and the remainder will mostly be assigned to the fast track (where written expert evidence alone is admissible). But those worth more than £15,000 could be allocated to the multi-track. If that happens, you may eventually be required to give evidence from the witness box and be cross-examined on it.

Most criminal cases proceed to trial

In contrast, except when a defendant pleads guilty, all criminal cases will result in a trial and the expert can expect to be called to give oral evidence. Similarly, court appearances are more common in family proceedings.

In other circumstances you may be asked simply to investigate and provide a preliminary report to assess the strength of the case. Should that result in the matter being taken no further, there will be nothing more for you to do.

Consider the implications of moving from expert advisor to expert witness

Between these two extremes there is a host of ways in which you might become involved.

- The request for a preliminary report could well be followed by one for a **full report** destined for exchange and possible use in court.

- You might be asked to take part in a **meeting of experts**.
- After reports have been exchanged, you may well be asked for a **technical assessment** of the report prepared by the opposing expert.

It is normal to comment on other expert reports

- At trial, you may be asked to **advise counsel** on the weaknesses to be probed in cross-examination.
- Finally, you may be required to provide further **technical back-up** should the case go to appeal.

As can be seen, expert witnesses can have several roles to play, and there are many permutations of these roles. The potential extent of your involvement in a case may well not be apparent from the instructions received at the outset.

An expert can play several roles in a case

5.5 Acceptance of instructions

If, after receiving instructions and clarifying any details of doubt, you are prepared to accept the assignment, acceptance should always be confirmed in writing. To avoid any possibility of confusion, it would be as well to use this opportunity to:

Acceptance should be in writing

- set out your **understanding** of the issues to be covered in the report(s)
- give a **timetable** for producing the report(s)
- specify whatever **other information** you require before a start can be made
- confirm that no **conflicts of interest** have been identified, and
- confirm the task is **within your expertise**.

5.6 Provision of documents

List all documents you considered in the report

The solicitor's letter of instruction should have listed the documents in his possession that will be sent to you on acceptance of the assignment. Any document, or verbal instruction, of any relevance to your expert opinion will need to be referenced in your written report.

Beware any request to treat a document as being 'for background only'

You should be particularly alert to any attempt by the solicitor, when forwarding a document, to claim that it is provided for background only and should not be relied upon or mentioned in any report prepared for exchange or use in court. If a document is material to your opinion it must be referenced in your report.

Medical doctors should obtain consent to access medical records

In the case of medical records, it may be that these are still held by the hospital or the client's general practitioner. In this case it is possible that you may have to apply to see them. At the very least, though, the solicitor should be able to state where the records are located and provide evidence that the client/patient has given consent for their disclosure.

The lawyer has a duty to provide you with all relevant documents

In general, the solicitor should respond promptly to any requests from you for further information. Without prompting, the solicitor ought also to send copies of all documents, witness statements, pleadings, etc., disclosed by the other side that may have a bearing on the issues on which you will be reporting.

You can anticipate being given a copy of the other side's report

Finally, on exchange of reports, the solicitor has a duty to inform you when exchange took place and to send a copy of the report prepared by the expert for the other side(s). The latter is essential because it:

- may reveal information or raise issues that might make you wish to **change an opinion** expressed in your report, or

- may prompt a rejoinder in the form of a **supplementary report**.

As a matter of courtesy, the solicitor ought also to keep you posted on the progress of the case, including any amendments to the pleadings that are relevant to your opinion. Experience shows this to be a duty more often observed in the breach!

Lawyers tend to be poor at keeping experts abreast of developments

However, in the civil justice system, the CJC Experts Protocol does now require your lawyer to provide copies of court directions that relate to you.

Your lawyer must provide you with copies of court directions

5.7 Record, retain, reveal

In the aftermath of the *Sally Clark* case, the CPS developed a good practice guide for expert witnesses instructed by prosecuting authorities in criminal cases. Despite this narrow origin, its content is worth noting by expert witnesses working in all types of proceeding.

The key point it addresses is the need for you always to **record, retain and reveal all the evidence considered when arriving at an opinion**. This includes any evidence you consider but subsequently conclude is not relevant to the opinion formed.

Reveal all the evidence considered, even if you think it is irrelevant

The logic underlying this rule is that while you may conclude that some evidence is not relevant to your opinion, you are not in a position to say it has no relevance in the wider context of the litigation.

5.8 Draft and final reports

An instructing solicitor will usually ask you to submit your report intended for exchange in draft form. The purpose of this is not, as some might suppose, to have you alter it better to support the client's case. It is to ensure that:

A request for a draft report is quite normal

Your lawyer will check for any technical omissions

- the **report meets the requirements of the court** (to which, in any case, it has to be addressed), and in particular those requirements as to its content which are specified in the relevant rules and practice directions (see *Appendices 2–6*), and

Your lawyer will check report structure

- the **report is organised in a way that will facilitate your examination-in-chief** should a court appearance subsequently be required.

With these considerations in mind, the aspects of the report on which the solicitor will most want to focus while it is still in draft form are as follows.

- Does it contain the basic minimum of **information about you and your credentials** for writing the report, **the case** to which it relates and **the party** on whose behalf it has been prepared?

The report must include the substance of all instructions

- Does it state accurately the **substance of all instructions** received by you, whether written or oral, on the basis of which the report has been written?
- Does it **fulfil the brief** given?

Where relevant, the report should also:

- give details of the **technical literature** or any other material on which you have relied
- provide all necessary **background information** for an understanding of the investigations undertaken or the methodology used

The report must make clear if others contributed

- state **who conducted the tests and experiments** (if any) you have used for the report and their qualifications for carrying them out
- set out the **facts ascertained** and the **inferences drawn** from them, with convincing reasoning for doing so

- analyse, and if possible account for, any **contradictions** that may have emerged in the course of fact gathering or were revealed in documents disclosed by the other side.

In any event, the solicitor will wish to ensure that:

The report must clearly separate facts from opinions

- the report **summarises your findings**
- the report **provides a clear statement of opinion** as to what happened (or will happen) and/or why it happened (or will happen), and
- all expressions of opinion are confined to **matters within your competence**.

If any question should have arisen as to whether what was done conformed to normal practice, the report should:

- **identify any relevant recognised body of opinion** regarding normal practice which differs from yours, and
- **give your reasons for the opinion**.

Finally, the solicitor will wish to check that the report satisfies two specific requirements, namely that it:

The required statement of truth must be included

- **concludes with a statement** to the effect that you understand your duty to the court and have complied with that duty, and
- **is verified by a 'statement of truth'** in the form laid down.

5.9 Answering written questions

CPR provides for written questions to be put to experts

Written questions to an expert are allowed in all civil proceedings. There is no provision for written questions to experts in criminal proceedings.

In civil cases, the main purpose of putting written questions to experts is to help the parties understand the reports disclosed to them. The court may disallow the questions and make an appropriate order for costs against the party putting them if:

Permission to answer should be sought from your instructing lawyer

- questions are put that are **oppressive in number or content**, or
- without the permission of the court or the agreement of the other side, questions are asked for any purpose other than **clarification** of the expert report.

When you receive written questions you should:

- check with your instructing solicitor(s) that you have his **permission to answer** them
- ensure you follow the appropriate **rules of disclosure** relating to your role in the proceedings (see §5.9.2).

5.9.1 Should you answer?

Once permission is granted, you can answer

Your solicitor will want to check that the questions have been **properly put**. For a question to be properly put, it must conform to the requirements of CPR 35.6(2) (see *Appendix 2*).

If jointly instructed, you should only receive questions that have already been circulated to all the parties. Nonetheless, you would be wise to ensure that all the parties agree to your answering any questions put to you.

If permission is given by your instructing solicitor(s), you can consider and answer the questions.

5.9.2 Disclosure

Be clear who should be sent copies of your answers

- In family proceedings, all your answers must be disclosed to all parties.
- When acting as an SJE in civil proceedings, your answers to an agreed set of questions must be forwarded to all parties simultaneously.

- When acting as a party-appointed expert in civil proceedings, you should return your answers to the enquiring party, copying them to your instructing solicitor.

5.9.3 Who pays?

If you are a party-appointed expert, then your instructing solicitor will be responsible for payment of your fees for answering written questions. This is so, even though it is an opposing party asking the questions.

If you are an SJE, then all parties are jointly and severally liable for your fees. You should ensure at the outset of an SJE instruction that you address the issue of payment. Do you need to split invoices equally between the parties (and thus have multiple bills to chase), or will one party agree to be invoiced?

5.10 Summary

Ensure you comply with the relevant rules of court

It's clear that whatever system you are working under, an expert's deskwork will follow broadly similar requirements. Court-specific guidance is set out in the relevant rules and regulations as follows:

- for **criminal work**, refer to Rule 33.3 of the CrimPR (see *Appendix 5*)
- for **civil work**, read Rules 35.5, 35.6 and 35.10 of the CPR and relevant parts of the associated Part 35 Practice Direction which incorporates the CJC's Protocol for the Instruction of Experts to give Evidence in Civil Claims (see *Appendices 2–4*)
- for **family work**, read the information pertaining to civil proceedings above and the new practice direction (see *Appendix 6*).

All these rules and guidance are reproduced in the appendices. They can also be viewed in full on-line at www.justice.gov.uk by following the relevant links, or in the Expert Library of the website of the *UK Register of Expert Witnesses* at www.jspubs.com.

Send an invoice with your final report; send another later if you answer written questions

Ideally an **invoice** should accompany your final report marked for the attention of your instructing solicitor, with the due date for payment marked clearly. An additional invoice should follow on thereafter if written questions about the report require answering.

6

Expert discussions and court work

Move away from your desk and a new skill set is needed

Whenever you take on a case you must be prepared, if necessary, to take part in expert discussions and make an appearance in court. While in the vast majority of civil cases your opinion will be restricted to your expert report, in criminal and family proceedings you'll be expected to appear in court on a much more regular basis.

Such face-to-face encounters require a different skill set to that needed for report writing, and your powers of oral communication and self-control could be tested severely. Training is available to refine your courtroom skills and provide added confidence. For details of training providers, see §3.4.1.

6.1 Expert discussions

All courts encourage pre-trial expert discussions

Expert discussions are encouraged in civil, criminal and family proceedings. The CPR and CrimPR both speak of discussions between experts rather than meetings, and clearly envisage contacts of a more informal nature. So discussions need not necessarily be face to face. They can take the form of:

Discussions can be face-to-face, over the 'phone or by letter/e-mail

- an **exchange of letters, e-mails or faxes**
- **video-linked meetings**, or
- **telephone conferencing**.

Expert discussions can take place at any time by arrangement between the parties. It is more often the case, though, that they are ordered by the court, i.e. after proceedings have been issued.

Constructive discussions identify areas of common ground

The majority of expert discussions are constructive and help to identify substantial areas of common ground. The general view of those who have taken part in one is that they are 'a good thing'. At the very least they serve to establish the extent of agreement and disagreement on technical issues, and they may help resolve some differences.

Discussions focus attention on deciding areas of agreement and disagreement

In fact, it is quite likely that if the experts for both (or all) sides have been working from the same basic information, there will be much common ground. In such circumstances it should be possible for the experts to agree matters not in dispute without too much difficulty, while leaving areas of differing opinion, such as interpretation, degree and quantum, to be resolved. That, in turn, should enable the experts – and ultimately the court – to focus their attention on the issues that are actually in dispute, with consequent savings in time and effort.

However, expert discussions can prove a complete waste of time if the experts taking part have been told by their instructing solicitors not to agree anything without first obtaining clearance from them.

Lawyers like the insights discussions provide but fear losing control

The attitude lawyers take towards expert discussions is often distinctly ambivalent. They **welcome the insight** such meetings can afford into the strengths and weaknesses of their own case and that of the opposing side. But they are **fearful of losing control** of any aspect of their client's case, however technical it might be.

6.1.1 Discussions arranged by the parties

'Voluntary' discussions are uncommon

Parties adducing expert evidence have always been free to arrange discussions between their experts. This has never become general practice, it having more to do with a desire to hide one's hand until the last possible moment than to any other consideration. Those discussions that are held generally take place in the context of negotiated settlements and often during the course of the trial.

There are no rules governing expert discussions of this kind beyond those the parties themselves devise for the occasion. The scope of the discussions can be as narrow or as wide as the parties choose, and the parties may give the experts as much authority

The presence of lawyers is often counter-productive

as they like. It could be that the experts will be asked to settle a single technical issue, while at the other extreme they might be instructed to try to bring about a settlement. Although the instructing solicitors can, if they wish, arrange to be present throughout a discussion, this is undesirable. It tends to:

- **inhibit the freedom of dialogue** between the experts and
- **restrict the effectiveness** of their discussions.

It is far better for the lawyers to impose a requirement that they be consulted before any agreement is concluded.

You must understand the role you are to play

As discussions arranged by agreement are not governed by any rules of court or settled practice, it is especially important that the experts taking part in them ensure they are fully briefed as to the role they are to play. They will also need to inform the other experts involved:

- of any **restrictions** that have been placed upon their authority, and
- whether their participation is conditional on the proceedings being '**without prejudice**'.

6.1.2 Court-ordered discussions

Court-ordered discussions are not meant to decide issues

The function of a court-ordered discussion is not to decide anything – for that is the responsibility of the court – but to enable the experts who have been instructed in the case:

- to **discuss the technical issues** it poses that are within their expertise and
- to **exchange opinions** on them.

Expert discussions are usually held after exchange of the reports, but there is nothing to prevent a discussion being arranged before reports have been written. Indeed, a pre-report discussion could well result in clarification of the issues to be addressed, exchange of more focused reports and subsequent savings in court time and costs.

Court-ordered discussions focus attention on the real matters in dispute

An expert discussion should result in:

- a **pooling of technical information** regarding the case
- the **identification of any gaps in that information** which may need to be filled, and
- a **narrowing of the areas of difference**, some of which may at least be the result of a misunderstanding or lack of data.

Official guidance

Court rules govern such discussions

Specific guidance for pre-hearing discussions between experts is offered in the official rules and practice directions for civil, criminal and family proceedings.

- **Family proceedings** – see Rules 6.2–6.5 of the Practice Direction: Experts in Family Proceedings relating to Children (see *Appendix 6*).
- **Civil proceedings** – see section 18 of the CJC's Protocol for the Instruction of Experts to give Evidence in Civil Claims (see *Appendix 5*) and Rule 35.12 of the CPR (see *Appendix 2*).
- **Criminal proceedings** – see Rule 33.5 of the CrimPR (see *Appendix 5*).

Directions

It is for the court to decide whether to order an expert discussion. In the exercise of its case management function it may do so at any stage in the proceedings.

The court may set the agenda, but often it does not

It is also for the court to decide when the discussion should take place. It may require that the experts make contact before exchange of their reports or after exchange. Alternatively, the court may leave the timing of the discussion to be settled by the parties. Similarly, the order can be quite detailed about the issues the experts are to address, or mention none at all.

Who takes part?

Discussions are often restricted to experts of like discipline

Experts obviously take part in expert discussions, but they are not necessarily joined by all of those involved in the case. Where experts have been instructed to deal with different aspects, the court may order discussions between 'experts of like discipline'. On grounds of cost alone there are clear advantages in that.

On the other hand, while this limitation will be desirable in most cases, it may not be so in all of them. For example, in actions for clinical negligence it has been found that when experts on breach of duty and those on causation meet, the interchange of views can go a long way towards determining where the real issues in the case lie.

Should lawyers take part?

Lawyers will not usually be present; if present, they should be passive

Lawyers will not normally take part in an expert discussion unless all the parties and their experts otherwise agree or a court so orders. If involved, lawyers should only answer questions put to them by the experts or advise about the law.

Details of all discussions are private

The involvement of lawyers may inhibit some experts from making a full and frank contribution to the discussion, perhaps out of concern that the ideas they float might be used against them in cross-examination. Although the various rules provide that anything said in the course of an expert discussion may not be referred to in court, it still leaves open the possibility that a lawyer listening to the discussion might glean from it additional ways of probing an expert's evidence and undermining his confidence in the witness box.

Against this, it has to be said that expert discussions can get derailed easily for other reasons. For example:

- **an inexperienced expert so far defers to the views of other senior experts** in the case as to completely abandon the opinions advanced in his original report

You should not be swayed from your opinion by the seniority of an opposing expert

- **both experts may be so inclined to compromise** that the agreed statement produced fails to reflect the views of either of them
- **one or both experts may assume the role of advocate for the client** and even usurp the function of the court in deciding where blame lies in the case.

You should never become an advocate for 'your side'

In all these circumstances, if the lawyers for the parties were involved in the discussions, they would (hopefully) intervene to prevent such an outcome and get the discussion back on track.

One further point made by litigation lawyers is that it is they, not the experts, who represent the interests of their clients. In their view it is wholly unreasonable that the outcome of a case should be determined, as it is quite often, by a statement produced at the end of an unmonitored discussion between two experts, one of whom may well not have met their client and who, in the context of legal proceedings, owe the client only a secondary duty of care. If the lawyers monitored the discussion, even though they are debarred from taking part in it, they could at least exercise a watching brief on their client's behalf.

When should discussions be held?

The court can set the timing of a discussion

The court itself may require that the ordered expert discussion takes place before or after exchange of the reports. The circumstances of the case and the facts to be established by expert evidence largely determine which stage is preferred.

Given the choice, most experts would like discussions to take place sooner rather than later. If experts can agree the issues not in contention early on, then they need not be covered in detail in the reports yet to be written. That, in turn, should reduce the amount of material the court has to consider and ultimately costs.

On the other hand, and especially in complicated cases, opportunities for meaningful discussions may be missed if experts hold an expert discussion before all have had the chance to complete their own investigations and at least draft a preliminary report. To be involved in a discussion without having any prior knowledge of the technical basis of the opposing side's case can prove very frustrating.

Discussions after reports have been exchanged can be limiting

There can be even greater disadvantages, though, in requiring expert discussions after final reports have been exchanged.

- Experts will have completed their investigations by that stage (and, quite conceivably, incurred most of their expenses).
- Experts are likely to be less willing to change opinions expressed in their reports, either out of embarrassment at having to acknowledge the superiority of another viewpoint or because the reports will by then have been accepted by their clients as the basis on which to proceed.
- In the event of the discussion achieving its purpose, there will be a need to apply to the court

for permission for the experts to amend their reports or submit supplementary versions.

Where should discussions be held?

Experts now have much more flexibility in terms of scheduling expert discussions, and the courts can benefit from the resultant cost savings.

Flexibility is the key – most experts have very full schedules

The principal consideration in choosing the venue for a face-to-face expert discussion is that it should be convenient for the majority of those attending. It could be held at:

- the offices of one of the experts
- the office of one of the instructing law firms
- in a private room at a local hotel or conference centre.

Whichever location is chosen, it is essential that the meeting is held in private, with access to telephones, faxes and a computer/printer.

Preparation

If expert discussions are to fulfil their purpose, it is essential that an agenda is agreed in advance. Depending on the type of proceeding, the agenda may be drawn up by:

An agenda should be agreed in advance

- **all the parties** with joint agreement
- **the court**, but usually only if the parties cannot decide between themselves
- **the lead solicitor** in a joint instruction
- usually the **claimant solicitor** in a civil proceeding
- usually the **solicitor acting for the child** in a family proceeding
- usually the **prosecution** in a criminal case.

Who writes the agenda depends on the nature of the case

Conduct

Often experts will be left to conduct the meeting

The detailed arrangements for holding an expert discussion are normally left to the experts themselves.

- If more than two experts are involved, it is advisable that one should act as the **chairperson**.
- Whoever acts as the chair should conduct the proceedings in as **relaxed and informal** a manner as the circumstances allow.
- If the discussion is following an agenda or aide memoire, the chairperson must ensure that **each expert involved is called upon to speak** and given every opportunity to do so.

Try hard to overcome any hostility in a fellow expert

Occasionally, experts will find that one of their number adopts a hostile or uncooperative stance. If that attitude persists, it could ruin any chances of a successful outcome. It is then incumbent on the other experts involved to overcome the problem as far as possible and to attempt to win that expert round. Most individuals will respond to tactful handling and a show of flexibility on the part of their fellow professionals.

Another tack might be to abandon the agenda and concentrate on those issues most easily resolved, hoping thereby to progress to the more difficult ones when some measure of mutual respect has been gained.

The worst an implacably hostile expert can do is to prevent agreement being reached

But remember, the purpose of the meeting is to *try* to identify the areas of agreement and disagreement. If a hostile expert cannot be brought round, the meeting will have to conclude that no agreement could be reached.

What is essential, even if the court has not required it, is that minutes are kept of the discussion. If at all possible, a statement should be drawn up at the end of the discussion setting out the agreed answers to the questions posed by the agenda. It should be signed and dated by all involved.

The statement should detail:

Aim to create an agreed joint statement

- those **issues on which the experts agree**, with a summary of the reasons for agreement, and
- those **issues on which the experts disagree**, with a summary of the reasons for disagreement.

In addition, the statement should include a list of further issues identified during the discussion but not on the agenda, and a record of any further action the experts agreed was needed to resolve these and any other outstanding issues.

Status of the joint statement

A joint statement is for the court's use

All conversations that take place at court-ordered expert discussions are privileged. But any joint statement drawn up at the end of a discussion is for the court's use. It is an 'open' document. Although it may not be binding on the parties, it should prove invaluable to the court in its subsequent management of the case.

The 'open' nature of the statement has one other major consequence. An expert could hardly submit evidence to a court that was contrary to what was agreed at an expert discussion ordered by the court – unless, that is, new information had come to hand that justified a change of mind.

This could place the expert's instructing party in a real quandary if it is unwilling to abide by the statement of issues agreed following the expert discussion. All the more reason, then, why the practical aspects of expert discussions deserve the most careful attention of everyone involved in them.

Expert's position post-discussion

You cannot be cross-examined on what happened during an expert discussion

What is quite clear is that **nothing discussed or agreed during the course of a 'without prejudice' expert discussion may be disclosed in court**. It follows that should an expert who has taken part in such a discussion come to give his evidence in court, he cannot be cross-examined about the discussions or, more to the point, any inconsistencies between the evidence-in-chief and what may have been stated or agreed during the discussion.

That said, it would clearly be wrong for an expert to give evidence at trial contrary to what was previously said or agreed at an expert discussion – unless, that is, fresh evidence has been discovered or a genuine change of mind has occurred.

Party's position post-discussion

By the same token, the party whose expert agrees at a 'without prejudice' discussion matters contrary to that party's pleaded case has very limited options.

- The party may choose to **concede all or part of its case**.
- The party can **seek leave to amend its statement of claim**.
- The party can **dispense with the services of its expert**.

Conclusion

Expert discussions can be very useful at narrowing the issues in dispute

While it may be that some uncertainties remain about the status and effect of agreements reached by experts taking part in court-ordered discussions, this should not be allowed to detract from an appreciation of the overall usefulness of such discussions. They serve:

- to **focus the attention** of both the experts and those instructing them on the technical issues that really matter
- to **narrow the issues** in dispute, and
- to **promote early settlement** of the case.

Even when settlement does not occur, such discussions should at least result in the experts producing shorter, better focused reports, with all the consequent savings in court time that will follow. Since cost has always been one of the principal bugbears of litigation, this alone would be a sufficient justification for the wider use of expert discussions.

6.2 Preparing for court

Take time to prepare for a court appearance

Any appearance in court will require careful preparation at your desk. All documents should be reviewed and reports re-read. With the benefit of time, any new lines of enquiry that suggest themselves should be discussed with your instructing solicitor. However, it is highly unlikely that any further investigation will be authorised at such a late stage.

You should...

- check the **time and location** of the trial
- make **travel plans** well in advance, choosing the most economic route
- ensure that your instructing party is fully aware of any **expenses** you are likely to incur so that, should settlement be reached, they can be included in any agreement
- spend time in advance **re-reading your report** and associated notes
- ensure that **all documents and other items required to give your evidence are together in one place** ready for your journey to court

Attention to detail will help keep pressure on the day to a minimum

- find out the **name and titles of the presiding magistrate(s) or judge(s)** so that you can use their correct form of address in court (see below)
- remind yourself of **court etiquette**
- make sure that your **personal appearance** is commensurate with your professional role in the proceedings
- decide which **form of oath** is suitable for you and your beliefs.

6.2.1 Forms of address

Don't embarrass yourself by demoting the judge!

Before attending court it is worth making some effort to find out who will be presiding over the case and their title. There are correct forms of address that should be adopted, and they are detailed below.

Who	Correct form of address
Magistrate	Sir or Madam or Your Worship
District judge	Sir or Madam
Circuit judge, recorder or assistant recorder	Your Honour
Registrar	Sir or Madam
High Court Master	Master (regardless of gender)
High Court Judge	Your Lordship/Your Ladyship or My Lord/ My Lady
Lord Justice of Appeal	Your Lordship/Your Ladyship or My Lord/ My Lady
Lord Chief Justice (most senior criminal judge in England and Wales)	Your Lordship/Your Ladyship or My Lord/ My Lady

Form of address is not court-dependent

The form of address is not court-dependent. So, for example, a High Court Judge should be referred to as Your Lordship/Your Ladyship or My Lord/My Lady regardless of the court setting. If in doubt, or to be doubly sure, ask your instructing lawyer or a court usher for confirmation prior to the hearing.

You should avoid excessive use of these terms. It is probably sufficient to use them once to preface or end responses. It would be inappropriate and, frankly, laborious to use them in every sentence.

6.2.2 The courtroom

The constitution of the courtroom will depend on the type of case being heard.

Be familiar with the make up of the court

- In **civil proceedings** you could face a judge or a jury. A minority of civil cases (licensing and certain areas of family law) take place in the magistrates' court, where a panel of magistrates or a judge will govern proceedings.
- A panel of magistrates or a judge will preside over **criminal proceedings**, with indictable offences being heard in front of a jury.
- In **family proceedings** you'll present your evidence to a panel of specially trained magistrates or judges.

You should make sure that you understand the layout of the courtroom and the roles and responsibilities of the key players well in advance of your appearance.

6.2.3 Courtroom etiquette

Courtroom etiquette is just good behaviour

Courtroom etiquette is the same for expert witnesses as for any other person using or appearing in the court. Broadly speaking, these are merely rules of good behaviour and can be summarised as follows:

- **Remove all headgear** before entering the court. (There are exceptions for religious observances.)

- **Enter and leave the courtroom at an appropriate time** so as to cause as little disturbance as possible.
- When not giving evidence, **keep quiet at all times**.
- **Sit in the designated area**, which will be pointed out to you by the usher.
- **Stand when the judge enters or leaves** the court.
- Always **ask the usher if you are in any doubt** as to what to do.

Courts have bans on certain activities

The following activities are **not permitted** in court: smoking, eating and drinking, reading magazines and newspapers, taking photographs, making tape-recordings, using a mobile telephone or using a personal stereo. Animals are not permitted in court, except a guide dog accompanying a registered blind person.

6.3 Court attendance

Remember, you are non-partisan – unlike the lawyers

The expert in court has a special responsibility to assist the court in coming to a just conclusion. You should not be partisan and should not seek to hide matters that help or hinder one party or the other. This role is in contrast to that of the lawyers, who are partisan and whose questions will be designed to present a client's case to its best advantage.

Ensure your full opinion gets heard

Consequently, you should not be afraid to expand on a reply to a question and should not allow answers to be driven by the examining advocate. When in doubt, you should ask the judge for permission to offer a fuller explanation and, where necessary, to use visual aids and other materials if these will assist in presenting the evidence in a way that will be understood more easily.

In expressing your opinion, you should take into consideration all the material facts before the court at the time the opinion is expressed. If, for any reason, you are not satisfied that the opinion can be expressed finally and without qualification, you should indicate that the opinion is provisional or qualified, as the case may be.

If your opinion is in any way qualified, make sure the court knows

You should also take great care to confine your responses and opinions to matters that are material to the dispute between the parties and which relate only to matters that lie within your expertise. But it should be recognised that this 'knowledge boundary' is not one that is always clear-cut. Accordingly, you should make it clear to the court when a particular matter falls near the periphery of your area of expertise.

Always respect your 'knowledge boundary'

6.3.1 Taking the oath

You will be called by the court usher and asked to stand whilst taking the oath. The court views the taking of the oath as a grave matter. The Oaths Act 1978 makes provisions for the forms in which oaths may be administered and states that a solemn affirmation shall be of the same force and effect as an oath. As with other witnesses, you remain under oath until dismissed by the judge.

The oath is a grave matter

At the conclusion of the evidence the judge will usually thank and formally release you. You are then free to go but should not discuss the case with people outside the court. Usually, however, you will be required to assist the instructing legal team. This will frequently mean sitting behind counsel whilst the other side's expert is examined and answering any questions that may arise. You will often need to explain quite basic things about that evidence and will need to stay alert for any inaccuracies it might contain.

Once released from the stand, you will often be asked to assist counsel with the other experts

6.3.2 Civil trial format

In brief, a civil trial proceeds as follows:

1 Opening speech from claimant's advocate

2 Opening speech from defence team (occasionally)

3 Claimant witnesses give evidence
  For each witness in turn...
    Examination-in-chief by claimant team
    Cross-examination by defence team (if required)
    Re-examination by claimant team (if required)

4 Defence witnesses give evidence
  For each witness in turn...
    Examination-in-chief by defence team
    Cross-examination by claimant team (if required)
    Re-examination by defence team (if required)

5 Defence closing speech

6 Claimant closing speech

6.3.3 Criminal trial format

In brief, a criminal trial proceeds as follows:

1 Prosecution opening speech

2 Prosecution evidence called
  For each witness...
    Examination-in-chief by prosecution
    Cross-examination by defence (if required)
    Re-examination by prosecution (if required)

3 The defence now has the option to submit to the court that there is no case to answer if key elements of the case cannot be proved.

4 Defence opening speech

5 Defence evidence called
  For each witness...
    Examination-in-chief by defence
    Cross-examination by prosecution (if required)
    Re-examination by defence (if required)

6 Defence closing speech

7 Prosecution closing speech (optional) in the crown court, but rarely in the magistrates' court

Note that as an expert witness you can sit in court throughout the trial and listen to all the evidence adduced. Witnesses of fact are not permitted in the courtroom until after giving their evidence.

You can sit in court throughout the proceedings

6.3.4 Examination-in-chief

There is no set order in which a party should call its witnesses. Given that the evidence must follow some logical narrative sequence, it is probable that the witnesses of fact will be called first, followed by any expert evidence.

When called to give evidence, the advocate representing your instructing party will question you first. This is known as the **examination-in-chief**, the object of which is to elicit from you all material supporting the party's case.

Your own side will take you through your examination-in-chief

The examination-in-chief will usually begin with questions about your qualifications and experience and the methodology used in preparing the report.

Questions that are obviously steering you towards giving a particular response (known as **leading questions**) should not be asked in the examination-in-chief, except where there are uncontested facts and with the leave of the judge.

6.3.5 Cross-examination

The opposing side will cross-examine – but this isn't always necessary

After conclusion of the examination-in-chief the other party, or parties, will have the opportunity to put their own questions to you. This is known as **cross-examination**.

If you have not said anything to damage that party's case, or with which its own expert disagrees, there may be no need to cross-examine you at all.

Cross-examination can be hostile

When cross-examination takes place it may or may not be hostile in nature. You may simply be asked to expand on, or clarify, responses given in the examination-in-chief, or asked to state an opinion based on a slightly different hypothetical premise. However, the cross-examination may be an all-out attempt to discredit your evidence. This may be done by:

- making an **attack on your qualifications and credentials**
- adducing scientific literature containing authorities **contradicting your evidence**, or
- **attacking your opinion generally** and the methodology used.

You can be cross-examined about the basis of your opinion, regardless of whether this basis was canvassed under the examination-in-chief. You can also be asked to explain the significance of each step of the procedure followed.

Cross-examination can be very broad in its scope

As the scope for cross-examining of experts is much wider than it is for ordinary witnesses, the advocate might also ask you about:

- **materials not considered**
- **tests not conducted**, and
- **data not reviewed**,

as well as the implications of these.

Bear in mind that in cross-examination it is permissible to ask **leading questions**. The skilful advocate will often seek to take control by asking questions that require a simple 'yes' or 'no' answer.

Watch out for leading questions

The techniques the advocate might employ are many and various. These will range from the aggressive to the flattering, and may well involve questions designed to unsettle or cause a loss of temper or objective demeanour.

As unpleasant as it can be, however, cross-examination is seen as the most effective device:

Cross-examination may be unpleasant, but it has stood the test of time

- to **test the veracity of witnesses**
- to **expose the dishonest, mistaken or unreliable**, and
- to **uncover inconsistencies and inaccuracies** in oral testimony.

Cross-examination, by its very nature, is designed to produce answers that are favourable to the cross-examiner and cast doubt on the quality of your evidence. The 'golden rule' is to maintain a measured and calm approach.

Stay calm; getting emotionally charged won't help

If you find yourself in court, remember the following.

- You are there to **assist the court** and it is to the court that you owe your primary duty.
- **Take your time**, be deliberate and make sure you fully understand the question before giving your answer.
- **Be vigilant** for the ambiguous question that might have a double meaning or assumes an answer to an earlier question that you have not given.

Take your time, be vigilant and don't exaggerate

- If you don't understand the question, or if it seems ambiguous, **ask the advocate to repeat or clarify** it.
- **Don't be over-enthusiastic** and **don't exaggerate**; these traits can lead to suggestions of bias.

Be open and never lose your temper

- **Don't be evasive or aggressive**.
- **Never lose your temper**.
- **Maintain an objective approach** and acknowledge the existence of alternatives when it is reasonable to do so.
- **Don't be flippant** and never fence or argue with the advocate.
- **Try to be courteous**, no matter how irritated you might become.

Remember, it's not personal!

- Remember, **it's not personal**!

6.3.6 Re-examination and further questions

The judge and jury can also put questions to you

During the examination-in-chief or cross-examination, the judge might put questions to you. These will usually be designed to clarify an answer you have given or explore an area the judge considers particularly significant.

In the crown court, the jury, too, can put questions. These will be in the form of a written request to the judge.

After cross-examination has concluded, the party that originally called you may conduct a **re-examination**. They must, however, limit questions to clarifying only those matters arising during cross-examination. Leading questions may not be asked.

In some circumstances the court itself can recall a witness for further examination or cross-examination.

Indeed, in rare cases a party might be permitted to call evidence after it has closed its case to rebut evidence that was totally unforeseen.

6.3.7 Closing remarks

A first court appearance can be confusing and even intimidating. It is certainly not for the feint of heart. Even the experienced witness can find procedural matters bewildering at times. However, by correctly observing rules of conduct and court etiquette your path will be made somewhat easier.

7

Fees and getting paid

Payment problems abound, but lawyers are businessmen too

At every gathering of experts you'll hear tales of woe about unpaid invoices and bad debtors. Law firms will be named and individual lawyers noted. But since solicitors work in the law and are themselves businessmen, it can hardly be surprising that they will try to manipulate situations to their best advantage. If that means failing to remind you that you've still not managed to extricate a signed contract from them for a forthcoming assignment, then that's your problem not theirs.

Look out for your own interests while complying with the rules of court

Now there are solicitors who will do their utmost to ensure you work well together and everything is transparent, but they are few and far between. It is your responsibility to make sure you comply with all the relevant rules and regulations governing your work as an expert witness, while at the same time ensuring you keep business matters like fees and payment in focus and upfront.

Remember that an expert witness is paid for the time it takes to:

- **form an opinion** and, where necessary,
- **support that opinion** during the course of litigation.

Experts are paid for the time it takes to form an opinion, not for the opinion

An expert witness is *not* paid for the opinion given, and still less for the assistance that opinion affords the client's case. This underlines the independent nature of the role of the expert witness; you are not a hired gun.

7.1 Types of fee

Different fee scales should apply to different categories of work

There are several different types of fee you will need to consider:

- **secretarial work** you can safely delegate, e.g. typing, chasing records, etc., charged at a lower rate

- **research/investigative work** only you can do, charged at your usual rate
- **subcontracted work**, e.g. analytical tests, charged at cost
- **disbursements**, e.g. travel costs, accommodation expenses, medical record searches, photocopying, etc., charged at cost and subject to strict rules (see relevant legislation)

Disbursements are passed on at cost

- **cancellation** fees
- fees for answering **written questions**, charged at your usual rate
- fees associated with **expert discussions**
- **court attendance** fees.

Each will need unambiguous supporting documentation to make its ultimate collection as trouble-free as possible.

Keep proper records to justify your bills

7.2 Essentials

In addition, you will need to make sure that you:

- **insist that your solicitor signs the contract on behalf of his law firm**, making all the partners in the firm liable for your fee should he leave the firm

Use written terms and get them signed

- **have on file a signed copy of your contract** with the solicitor's law firm
- **have a transparent fee structure** so that your solicitor knows what to expect
- **agree a payment schedule** with your solicitor and have it confirmed in writing
- work with your solicitor to **ensure prior authority is gained** from his client (private or otherwise) before commencing any work

Find out if prior authority is required

Keep your lawyer appraised of ongoing costs

- **keep your instructing solicitor appraised of ongoing expenses** so that the size of an invoice is expected rather than a complete surprise
- **invoice promptly** on completion of a case or at agreed intervals during the case
- **send the invoice to the correctly named individual at the correct address**, including a case reference
- **make the expected payment date clear** on the invoice and provide as much supporting detail as possible with the invoice

Be prompt with your credit management

- **chase unpaid invoices promptly** with a polite telephone call (You will often find that the invoice has failed to reach its destination or is awaiting this very telephone call from you before being passed for payment.)
- **continue chasing the invoice for a set period**; if it remains unpaid, immediately **adopt your stated debt recovery procedures**
- **have a clause in your contract defining the procedures you will adopt should payment not reach you** within the given time period

Add a contractual duty to recover debt chasing costs

- **define in your contract exactly what charge you will add** to the invoice should payment fall overdue.

7.3 A contractual relationship

The expert–lawyer relationship is a contractual one

The starting point for any consideration of the payment of your fee is the contractual nature of the relationship between you and the instructing solicitor. It is the same regardless of the kind of case for which you have been (or are about to be) instructed or how the litigation is being funded. If you and the solicitor agree a fee (or the basis on which it is to be calculated) and the timing of its payment, the solicitor becomes contractually responsible for paying the fee in full and within the agreed time span. This is so even though:

- the **agreement may not have been put in writing** (although that obviously helps!)
- the **solicitor may not at that stage have been paid** by whoever is funding the litigation
- the **solicitor may not in the end recover the full cost** from whoever is funding the case.

Payments due under contract are not subject to a reduction by any third-party action

In none of these circumstances is there an implied term that you are prepared to accept whatever amount may be allowed, for example:

- on assessment of the costs of the case by the court, or
- by the LSC, should the defendant be legally aided, or
- from central funds for giving evidence in court in a criminal case.

Neither is there an implied term that you are prepared to wait for payment until conclusion of the case.

If a lawyer does not pay he should be sued

If the solicitor should default on his contractual obligations, you will generally be entitled to sue for the unpaid fees. The only reason why you might be deprived of that civil remedy is if it can be shown that the contract with the solicitor is void and unenforceable because it is contrary to statute law.

Your contract binds you as tightly as the lawyer

Of course, the contract binds you as much as the lawyer. If the lawyer can show that you have breached the contract in any way, then payment may be delayed, decreased or withheld. If such a situation occurs, then the mechanisms of dispute resolution specified in your terms and conditions will come into play.

Much more detail on contracts can be found in another book in this series, Little Book 1: *Expert Witness Fees*.

7.3.1 Limiting liability

Any limitation must be embodied in your contract

A solicitor wishing to limit liability to you in any of these ways, or to delay payment for any reason, must make it quite clear at the outset. It is then up to you to decide whether to agree to be instructed on such a basis.

Any shortfall on assessment should be borne by the lawyer, not you

Unless the solicitor has made this disclaimer, it follows that if all or part of your fee is not allowed on assessment of the costs of the case, the solicitor or the client must bear the deficit.

Assessment of costs by the court is about partitioning costs between the parties. A 'reduction in the expert's fee' only means a reduction in what one party can claim from the other. It does *not* mean you should be paid less, whatever the lawyer tries to tell you!

Naturally enough, solicitors dislike this situation – almost as much as experts dislike working on the basis that they will accept being paid whatever a court or a legal aid official may decide.

7.4 Conditional fee arrangements

CFAs make it difficult for lawyers to pay experts promptly

Unfortunately, the introduction of conditional fee arrangements (CFAs) as a way of funding a large swathe of civil actions has created a funding vacuum for disbursements, which includes the costs of expert reports.

In the past, privately funded civil cases rarely created payment problems for experts. The lawyer simply asked for 'payment on account' and so had ready access to client funds to meet the cost of an expert report. In CFA cases, though, there is an absence of funds until the case has settled. It is, then, unsurprising that in CFA cases many experts find that their lawyers become appallingly bad payers.

You are banned from taking part in CFAs

It is worth reinforcing here that on no account should you accept payment for your expert witness work on a conditional fee basis. This would make you reliant for your fee on the outcome of the case and thus subject to indefensible accusations of bias. Any expert evidence you submitted would be ruled inadmissible.

Regrettably, the rules hold back from a complete ban on conditionality. It is permissible for the timing of the payment of an expert to be based on the length of the case. So you could agree to be paid at the end of the case, when the lawyers are likely to have been paid themselves. What is absolutely barred, though, is any variation in the fee charged based on the outcome of the case.

7.5 Disbursements

Disbursements are out-of-pocket expenses

Disbursements are all those costs that you necessarily incur in carrying out the solicitor's instructions. They might include, for example, payments made for photography or the reproduction of maps and diagrams, and out-of-pocket expenditure on car mileage, taxi and rail fares, and hotel accommodation.

Take care: defined allowances apply in criminal cases

In criminal proceedings there are defined allowances available for you to cover disbursements associated with travel and accommodation. They are detailed in §7.7 below.

7.6 Civil work

Fee rates in civil cases are set by the market

In civil work (and family proceedings) you are free to negotiate a fee with your instructing party or parties. It is simply a matter of gauging the market and setting the fee appropriately. See *Appendix 1* for the latest expert witness fee survey. Use the data to help set your fee level.

Once you have a signed contract in place, there should be little problem enforcing the terms and conditions so long as you perform your duties to the satisfaction of the instructing party.

In civil and family cases, disbursements should be agreed with the instructing party before the cost is incurred. For the avoidance of any doubt, confirmation to proceed should be obtained in writing. The key is to ensure that the instructing party is fully aware of the value of any prospective invoice.

Create the right to cancellation fees through your contract

If the solicitor agrees a cancellation fee then the solicitor will become liable for payment of that fee in the event of the hearing:

- **taking less time** than expected
- **being postponed**, or
- **being cancelled** altogether.

This would be so, regardless of whether the solicitor is able to recover the cancellation fee on subsequent assessment of the costs of the case.

Moreover, in civil cases funded by the LSC, if there should be any shortfall in that respect, it is the solicitor who must pick up the tabs, because regulations paralleling those governing legal aid in criminal cases prohibit the client or anyone else from doing so.

7.7 Criminal work

Public funding is the norm in criminal cases

In many criminal cases the defendant will be granted legal aid, and so the LSC becomes the sole paymaster (see §7.8 Legal aid on page 163 below). To ensure payment, it is desirable for the instructing solicitor to obtain **prior authority** from the LSC for expert fees.

Experts instructed by the prosecution are slightly better off than defence team experts. They will be paid by whichever prosecuting authority has issued the instruction, e.g. the CPS, a local police authority, etc. Expert witness fees for the prosecution are currently not fixed; the fee is negotiated for each appointment.

Prosecution experts fare better than defence experts

7.7.1 Court appearances for the defence

As a matter of public policy, if you are a defence expert witness in a criminal case you are entitled to be compensated out of central funds for your loss of time and the incidental expenses incurred in attending court. This applies whether or not the defendant is legally aided.

Uniquely, defence experts appearing in criminal trials are paid out of central funds, regardless of their contract

Attendance fees

If you are a defence expert witness there is recognition that you are attending court not out of public duty but in your line of business. For that reason, while the regulations provide that you may receive the same travel and overnight expenses as other witnesses, they do not set a ceiling amount for your allowances for attending court. Instead, the court personnel, called 'determining officers', whose job it is to assess claims for witness allowances, are issued with guidance by the MoJ as to the appropriate levels of compensation for expert witnesses. This guidance was last revised in July 2003. It is set out in *Appendix 9*.

Official MoJ fee guidelines do not set a ceiling for expert witness fees

To quote the guidance:

> *'The rate bands cover a wide [range] of skill and, in some cases, a number of different kinds of skill. They provide neither a minimum nor a maximum*

limit, merely a guide to the level of allowances in normal circumstances. It may be appropriate, having regard to the particular circumstances of the case, to depart from the guidance scales. Such occasions will, however, arise exceptionally.'

The attendance fee actually paid is supposed to reflect the total time involved that day, including travelling time and waiting time. Moreover, it should be adjusted upwards if an exceptionally long journey had to be undertaken or attendance stretched well beyond the court's normal sitting time.

Where attendance in court involves only normal preparatory work (which is taken to mean up to 1 hour), it is usual to pay you an attendance fee inclusive of this. If, however, the preparation took longer than 1 hour, a separate payment for this may be made at a rate within the appropriate band and documentary evidence will be required.

You should note, though, that if you have already written a report on the case for which you have been, or are being, paid separately, this will be deemed to reduce the amount of work needed to prepare for the hearing in court.

Travelling expenses

Travel expenses can be reclaimed

In addition to attendance fees, you will usually be able to claim travelling expenses. There is a presumption, though, that public transport will be used where possible. This could include air travel if there is no reasonable alternative, or it is more economical in the long run (i.e. after taking account of savings in allowances that would become payable if air travel was not used). In such circumstances, though, you would be expected to take advantage of the cheapest fare. If, on the other hand, a rail journey is preferred, you may travel first class if the journey can be used for trial preparation.

In cases of urgency, or where no alternative means of transport is available, you may use taxis or hired cars and be reimbursed for the full cost of doing so and of tipping the driver. Without such an excuse, though, you will be paid only the equivalent cost for making the same journey by public transport.

There's a presumption that the cheapest form of transport will be used

Broadly speaking, the same applies if you decide to travel to court in your own car. The amount paid is calculated on a mileage basis rather than on actual or equivalent costs. The standard rate (currently set at 45p per mile, MoJ Guidance to Determining Officers; see *Appendix 9*) is payable only where use of a private car was:

- **necessary** (e.g. because no other means of travel was available or you have a disability)
- **reasonable** (e.g. because you were bringing exhibits), or
- **cheaper in the long run** (e.g. because use of public transport would have made it necessary for you to stay overnight and thereby become eligible for the extra allowances detailed below).

In such cases, too, you are entitled to be reimbursed for any **parking fees** or **congestion charges** incurred. If, however, you choose to travel by car when the court being attended is reasonably accessible by public transport, the travelling expenses will be calculated on the average cost of public transport – currently taken to be 25p per mile; parking fees and congestion charges will not be reimbursed.

Overnight allowances

As might be expected, you are not entitled to either the financial loss or daily subsistence allowances payable to 'ordinary' witnesses. You may, however, be eligible for an overnight allowance should you be

Basic overnight allowances are available

required in court on successive days. In August 2001 this was set at:

- £85.25 per night if the court is within the city centres of London, Birmingham, Manchester, Leeds, Liverpool or Newcastle-Upon-Tyne, or
- £55.25 if it is anywhere else.

In June 2005 an additional £21 per night subsistence allowance and a £5 personal incidental allowance were added. All these allowances apply only to hotel accommodation. If staying with family or friends, the rate payable is £25 per night.

Collecting court payments

Defence experts appearing in court can get paid immediately after the trial

One plus point about giving expert evidence for the defence in criminal cases is that, providing:

- you can **create an invoice** (including VAT, if appropriate) at the court
- **the claim falls within the MoJ's rate band** for your profession, and
- **the claim is regarded by the determining officer as reasonable**

then in most crown courts you should be able to collect the fee and allowances due at the court's cash office once you have finished giving your evidence.

Help the court understand why you should be paid more

And what can be done to influence the determining officer to pay at the best possible rate within the appropriate band? Well, for a start:

- you should **be as specific as possible about the amount of time spent** preparing for the hearing, and any equipment used or technical help enlisted
- if you are the **only expert witness in your field for miles around**, then say so

- if you are not the only one, then be sure to include in the claim **details of your experience and qualifications** to give the determining officer a 'feel' for your eminence and the inevitability of your selection to give expert evidence, and
- you should **provide full details of your travelling expenses** and any parking fees incurred in attending court.

7.7.2 Court appearances for the prosecution

If working for the prosecution, you will need to invoice your paymaster for your court appearance and associated expenses.

CPS publishes guidance on the cost of experts

It is most likely that you will be instructed by the CPS. So produced below is a summary of Costs Annex 3a – Experts, Professionals and Interpreters Fees, effective from 1 May 2005. It gives guidance on allowable travelling expenses and overnight allowances for expert witnesses instructed by the CPS. The only advice given relating to fees is as follows:

> *'Expert witness fees are not fixed; the fee is negotiated for each attendance. Expert witnesses should contact the CPS Area Office for advice.'*

Travelling expenses

- **Public transport** – Bus, train and tube fares will be reimbursed at standard (i.e. second) class fares. Exceptionally, first class fares may be reimbursed if it was necessary to undertake preparation work on the journey.
- **Cars** – The mileage rate for cars is 25p per mile. This is set so that it is roughly the same as the cost of public transport. Doctors are entitled to a higher rate, and other witnesses may be eligible for the higher rate if they can show that it was

necessary to use their own car (for example, because no public transport was available or there was a considerable saving of time and money).

- **Motorcycles** – Similar rules apply if you use your own motorcycle. The rate per mile paid is 23.8p. Exceptionally, higher rates may also be paid for motorcycles if you can show it was necessary to use your own vehicle instead of public transport.
- **Car parking** – Car parking charges will only be paid if you can demonstrate that it was necessary to use your own motor vehicle.
- **Taxis** – Taxi and other hired vehicle fares (including any reasonable tips) will only be paid in the case of emergency or where no other public transport was available.
- **Other transport** – If you intend to use some other form of transport (e.g. airplane), you are advised to contact the Area Cashier of the CPS for advice as to whether the cost will be reimbursed.

Overnight allowances

CPS will pay for overnight accommodation where necessary

Where it is necessary for you to stay overnight, a fixed allowance is paid towards the cost of **meals, accommodation and other expenses**. The allowance is up to:

- either £85.25 attendance overnight in Inner London (within 5 miles of Charing Cross), Birmingham, Manchester, Leeds, Liverpool or Newcastle-Upon-Tyne, or
- £55.25 attendance overnight elsewhere.

The CPS will normally arrange the hotel accommodation and pay for it. Day subsistence is not paid to experts.

7.8 Legal aid

The public funding of cases, whether civil or criminal, does not alter the contractual nature of the solicitor–expert relationship, but it can affect it in other ways. In particular, it increases the risk that a solicitor may end up not recovering the full cost of instructing you on his client's behalf.

Public funding does not alter the core contractual relationship

Once litigants in civil cases have been granted a funding certificate (or, if defendants in criminal cases, a legal aid order), they are relieved of any further responsibility for paying the lawyers who will be representing them. Depending on their means, they may have to make a contribution towards the costs of their case, but that is all. To help ensure that they do not come under pressure to pay extra to their lawyers, the latter are prohibited from receiving any payment for the work they do on publicly funded cases other than from public funds.

Public funding prohibits the lawyer using any other source of funding

In general, this restriction on payments to lawyers also applies to any disbursements a solicitor might make while preparing a publicly funded case for trial. It would apply, for example, to any fees or expenses the solicitor agrees to pay you on the client's behalf. The danger for the solicitor is that if such expenditure were subsequently to be disallowed, either wholly or in part, on assessment of the costs of the case, then he alone would be liable for the difference. This is because:

This bar extends to the cost of instructing experts

- **you are entitled to be paid in full**, and
- **the solicitor is debarred from accepting any contribution**, whether from the client or anyone else, to make good the shortfall.

Solicitors, of course, would much rather not run the risk of having to meet any part of the cost of a client's case themselves. In many cases this risk can easily be avoided if you and the solicitor are both on the ball.

7.8.1 Obtaining prior authority for expenditure

Prior authority solves the problem

In civil cases, once a funding certificate has been granted to their clients, solicitors may seek prior authority for disbursements such as payment for your expert report or the tendering of expert evidence in court. Prior authority, naturally enough, cannot be given retrospectively.

Once granted, prior authority completely protects the disbursement

Before giving it, the LSC's Area Office will need some fairly detailed information about the fees you will be charging, and it will then set a ceiling figure. Providing:

- the **need for the report or evidence still exists** when the solicitor gives you the go-ahead to prepare it, and
- the **LSC's ceiling figure is not exceeded**

the solicitor then has an **absolute guarantee of full reimbursement** for the charges you eventually make.

If you find, once work has started, that for reasons not apparent earlier the job is either going to take appreciably longer to complete or requires more in the way of disbursements, the instructing solicitor may apply again to the Area Office for an authority with a higher ceiling figure. Alternatively, you and the solicitor can both take the chance that the excess expenditure will also be allowed on taxation of the solicitor's costs.

Similar provisions exist for securing the LSC's prior authority to incur expenditure on written reports and opinions needed in criminal and care proceedings.

It is worth noting that it is not mandatory to seek prior authority in any case, or in respect of any type of disbursement. It is purely a discretionary process designed to protect the solicitor on a detailed costs assessment.

No prior authority is required to incur costs in relation to obtaining a report from you or to court attendance by you if your instruction has been authorised by the court. Although the amount of your fees will be determined when the costs are assessed, the LSC will, in the absence of a relevant change in circumstances (affecting the need for or the costs of the work), follow the directions given by the court where it has given leave for you to undertake certain specified work and may have given a direction as to the apportionment of your costs.

Not being mandatory, you should always ask if prior authority has been obtained

In relation to Children Act cases, the LSC has specifically stated that it wishes to discourage applications for prior authority that may serve only to delay the instruction of an expert and the court timetable for the proceedings.

7.8.2 Payments on account

The regulations governing public funding in civil cases also provide for payments to be made on account of disbursements as soon as the liability for them is incurred. This also applies with criminal cases in the crown court, although here only if the solicitor has obtained prior authority to incur expenditure of £100 or more and the disbursement is of at least £100.

With prior authority in place, funds can be drawn down immediately

In many cases, then, solicitors simply do not have to carry the cost of instructing you until their bills have been paid by the LSC, any more than they can use this as an excuse for not paying you until their own bills have been assessed by the court. If your instructing solicitor knows in advance how much you will be charging for your report, there is absolutely no reason why he should not slap in an application to the Area Office and be in funds to pay for it by the time the report is presented. And if the solicitor has taken the precaution of obtaining prior authority to incur the expenditure, this can be done secure in the knowledge that there is no risk of any part of the fee being disallowed subsequently.

7.8.3 Failure to obtain prior authority

Prior authority is just a convenience

But what if the solicitor instructing you neglects to apply for prior authority to incur the cost of your report? Does this mean that he cannot be reimbursed for it from public funds?

Not at all. Providing it can be shown that the report was necessary for the proper conduct of the proceedings, the expenditure may still be allowed when the total costs of the case come to be assessed. The only sure consequence of a failure to apply is that the solicitor will be unable to secure a payment on account to settle your bill. Despite that, he still remains liable to pay your fee on time in accordance with whatever arrangement was originally agreed between you.

Another possibility, of course, is that the LSC may turn down the solicitor's application for prior authority, perhaps because the accompanying estimate lacks sufficient detail. There is no right of appeal against such a decision, but the solicitor is at liberty to resubmit the application with further particulars.

Prior authority can be refused

Should the application be refused on the ground that the fee you propose charging is too high, the solicitor's options are distinctly limited. He could:

- **re-negotiate the fee** with you
- **press on with instructing you** in the hope of being able to justify the expense when the costs of the case are assessed

- **seek to persuade you at this late stage to accept whatever fee for your services is eventually allowed** on assessment of the costs of the case.

If, for whatever reason, none of these options proves feasible, then in civil cases the only other course open to the solicitor is to find a cheaper expert. This is because, as we have already seen, lawyers conducting a publicly funded case may not ask the client, or indeed anyone else, to contribute to the cost of disbursements they make on their client's behalf.

An exception to this rule is allowed, though, if your report is needed for a criminal case. Should the LSC refuse prior authority in those circumstances, the defendant's solicitor would – in theory, at least – be free to utilise private funds to pay for it.

7.9 Getting paid

Terms ease the path to payment

Written terms do not guarantee that you will be paid on time, but they do make clear to the solicitor your expectations and requirements.

Basic sets of terms can be found and adapted to suit your needs

Templates and precedents for standard terms of business applicable to experts are generally available and may be adapted to suit requirements. For a base set of terms which can be manipulated to suit the needs of your discipline, read Little Book 1: *Expert Witness Fees*, another book in this series, or see *Appendix 7*.

Experts listed with the *UK Register of Expert Witnesses* should visit www.jspubs.com where the on-line Terminator application can be used to generate a standard set of terms.

In addition, some professional bodies (e.g. RICS) produce sample terms of engagement for their members and issue codes of practice in relation to their use.

Try adding an incentive for early settlement

If your contract does define a payment period, consider including some incentive to the solicitor to make payment early. This will most often be in the form of a percentage reduction in the fee for prompt settlement. For example, a 10% reduction for fees settled within 7 days will serve to focus the mind of the solicitor on the advantages to the client. It could also give a healthy boost to your own cashflow.

7.9.1 Charging interest

You have a statutory right to add interest and a lump sum penalty

The County Courts Act 1984 and the Late Payment of Commercial Debts (Interest) Act 1998 offer you a further weapon. Just as the reduction for prompt payment can act as a carrot, adding interest to the debt can provide the stick.

Since 7 August 2002, the **Late Payment of Commercial Debts (Interest) Act** applies to all commercial debts. Provision is made for interest to be added at **8% over the official dealing rate, together with a lump sum** (£40 on a debt below £1,000, £70 on those below £10,000 and £100 for those above). Interest starts to run once the contractual payment date has passed. Alternatively, the **County Courts Act provides for interest to be charged at the rate of 8%**.

Use your terms to reinforce the right

So, when crafting your terms, you should specify exactly which Act you will apply to any outstanding debt. Otherwise the lawyer will presumably opt for the County Courts Act to apply.

7.9.2 Sue

Before suing for your fees, try reasonable recovery steps

The CPR require that, before commencing proceedings to sue, the parties should have taken reasonable steps to resolve the matter. For our present purposes it is assumed that the debt you are seeking to recover is neither disputed nor challenged by the solicitor. The spirit of the CPR will have been satisfied by a request for payment, possibly followed by a formal letter of complaint. The latter, if written to the instructing solicitor, should also be copied to the firm's senior partner (a step that often pays dividends). Finally, a formal 'letter before action' should be sent:

Try writing to the senior partner

- **identifying the debt** by reference to date, invoice number and amount
- **providing the details of any contractual or statutory interest** to be claimed
- **giving notice that, in default of payment within a certain time, court proceedings will be commenced**.

A solicitor will recognise a formal letter before action, and this will often prompt the firm to make payment. No solicitor wants to have a court judgment registered against him nor to suffer embarrassment at his local county court. Such letters might carry more weight if written by another solicitor. Most lawyers will do this for a modest fee.

Claim Form

If all else fails, issue a small claim

If this fails, you can proceed to the issue of the Claim Form. In claims for the recovery of a specified sum of money, you should use a standard court form numbered N1. This can be found on the Court Service website at www.hmcourts-service.gov.uk by following the link to court forms, or it can be obtained by visiting your local county court office.

The court will issue and serve the claim on the solicitor and will send you notice of issue, stating the date by which the defendant must acknowledge the claim or lodge a defence.

If they ignore your claim, default judgment will be issued

The notice of issue will include a tear-off form that you can complete and return to the court if the defendant has neither defended the claim nor made payment within the time allotted. The court will then enter judgment in your favour and serve on the solicitor an order to pay.

Enforcing the judgment is, of course, a separate matter, but unless there is a genuine dispute, most solicitors will settle before you have progressed that far.

A 'do it yourself' claim can be as simple as that. If in doubt, the court staff are usually happy to assist with procedural matters, but not with matters of law. Attending at your court office is not dissimilar to a visit to your post office. It is a step that most will take with reluctance, but it may be your best option when all else has failed.

Little Book 1: Expert Witness Fees offers further guidance

For further information about suing your lawyer, read Little Book 1: *Expert Witness Fees*, another title in this series.

8

Business matters

Once your business is growing and instructions are starting to flow in you will find that most cases will follow a well-trodden and familiar path. You'll be able to prepare your reports and submit your invoices without any trouble. But as you become more experienced you will come across some issues that bear closer examination here.

8.1 VAT

Expert witness work is not exempt from VAT

Value added tax (VAT) is a tax on the final consumption of many goods and services in the UK. The supply of some goods and services is exempt from VAT. However, expert witness services are not exempt and are rated as standard (i.e. 17.5%).

Exceed the current turnover threshold and you will need to register

The goods and services upon which you are liable to pay VAT are called 'taxable supplies'. If your business turnover reaches the VAT registration threshold (£67,000 on 1 April 2008) in any 12 month period, it must be registered for VAT. The business must then charge VAT on all of its taxable supplies.

VAT registration threshold changes annually on 1 April

Historically the VAT registration threshold increases annually on 1 April. Visit Her Majesty's Revenue and Customs's (HMRC) website (www.hmrc.gov.uk) for a currently applicable value.

It is your responsibility to add the tax. The amount you'll have to pay to HMRC is the difference between your **output tax** and your **input tax**.

Input tax arises on what you buy

Inputs are the goods and services that come 'in' to the business – the things that you buy. Inputs will include stationery, telephone services and other professional services. Any VAT you pay to your suppliers when they supply goods or services 'into' your business can be reclaimed from HMRC. This is your 'input tax'.

Output tax arises on what you sell

Outputs are the goods and services that go 'out' from your business. Outputs will include the expert reports you supply for the courts. You charge VAT on the invoices for these, and this is called your 'output tax'. What you do is collect this VAT on behalf of HMRC and pay it back to them at the end of the VAT period (normally every 3 months, but by agreement it can be annually).

You pay the difference between your output and input taxes

The amount of VAT you send to HMRC is the amount you have collected from your customers (your 'output tax') less the amount you have paid to your suppliers (your 'input tax'). Of course, should you have paid your suppliers more VAT than you have collected, HMRC will reimburse you.

If you fail to register on time, you may be liable to pay HMRC both the VAT on your taxable supplies from the date you should have been registered, and a fine.

8.1.1 Recharging expenses

Don't charge VAT on VAT

If you incur expenses on behalf of a client and you are going to recharge them and they included VAT when you paid them (e.g. a hotel bill), then you must remember to deduct the VAT from the amount you paid before you include it on your invoice. You will then add the VAT to the expense when you add the VAT to your invoice total. This means that the VAT you paid to the hotel (an input VAT amount) will be offset exactly by the VAT you charge your client (an output VAT amount). So, in other words, **you don't charge VAT on VAT**.

8.1.2 Cash accounting

Cash accounting: pay your VAT once your bills have been paid

The cash accounting scheme allows you to account for VAT (output tax) on your sales on the basis of payments you receive rather than on tax invoices you issue. This is different from the normal rules that require you to account for VAT on your sales as they take place or as soon as you issue a VAT invoice, even if your customer has not paid you. (Note that you cannot apply the cash accounting scheme retrospectively to your business.)

However, if you choose to use the scheme, you can only reclaim the VAT incurred on your purchases (input tax) once you pay your supplier. Under the normal method of accounting for VAT you can reclaim VAT on purchases you make as soon as you receive a VAT invoice, even if you have not paid your supplier.

Cash accounting helps with cashflow

The scheme could help your cashflow because you do not have to pay VAT to HMRC until your customer has paid you. The scheme will be especially helpful if you give your customers extended credit or suffer a lot of bad debts!

However, the scheme may not give you any benefit if you:

- are usually paid as soon as you make a sale, or
- regularly reclaim more VAT than you pay.

If you find the scheme is of no benefit, you can leave it voluntarily at the end of a VAT accounting period and return to the normal method of accounting for VAT.

Full details of the scheme can be downloaded from the HMRC website (www.hmrc.gov.uk; HMRC reference: Notice 731).

8.1.3 Should you register voluntarily?

You can register voluntarily

Even if your annual taxable turnover is below the current VAT registration threshold, you may be eligible to apply for 'voluntary registration'.

There are advantages and disadvantages to registering voluntarily. Increased 'credibility' with customers is, says HMRC, one of the major benefits.

That may be so. But frankly, how many of your clients will notice the VAT number on your bill – still less be impressed by it? The most important benefit is that if your business makes standard or zero-rated supplies, you'll be able to reclaim your input tax.

VAT registration means you can claim all the VAT back on business supplies

Once you are registered, you are entitled to claim back VAT on the goods and services you buy in the course of your normal business activity. The categories of goods and services for which you can claim back VAT are as follows:

- **purchases for resale**
- **telephone bills** and **stationery**
- **capital items**, like office equipment for your business, and
- **meals with clients** in the course of business trips, unless the sole purpose for the trip was entertainment.

Partial VAT claims can be made for supplies used in your business and your home

In circumstances where goods or services are used for both business and private purposes you cannot recover VAT on all of these expenses, but only on the amount attributable to business use. For example, if you use a home telephone for professional as well as private purposes, you would need to apportion the business use element when calculating the proportion you are entitled to reclaim.

VAT can also be reclaimed on the costs of setting up your business

It is also possible, subject to certain conditions, to reclaim any VAT charged on goods or services that you use to set up your business. Normally this will include:

- VAT on goods you bought for your business within the last 3 years and which you have not yet sold, together with
- VAT on services you received not more than 6 months before your date of registration.

You should include this VAT on your first VAT return. Notice 700, The VAT Guide, gives more information on this.

You must maintain accurate and complete records

The main disadvantage to registration is simply the amount of extra work involved in keeping and maintaining the necessary records and accounts. You must keep records of all your business supplies and purchases. You will also need to keep a note of all the VAT you have charged and paid for each period covered by your VAT returns. If you are already in business you will probably find you can use your normal business records to provide this information.

If you currently employ an accountant to keep these records in proper order there are few operational reasons not to apply for VAT registration. However, once registered, you have a duty to make your records available for examination by HMRC. In addition, any of your customers who are not VAT registered will be unable to reclaim the VAT you start to add to your fees. You can find out more about what you need to do in Notice 700/21 Keeping Records and Accounts or by calling the HMRC helpline on 08450 109000.

8.1.4 The Flat-Rate Scheme

Simplified VAT regime for small businesses

The Budget of 2002 saw the introduction of the Flat-Rate Scheme as an alternative to the normal method of VAT accounting. Brought in to help small businesses, the Scheme allows eligible businesses to calculate their net VAT liability as a flat-rate percentage of their total turnover.

To enhance the simplicity further, the Flat-Rate Scheme can be used in conjunction with cash accounting – so you don't have to pay any VAT until your bills have been paid.

To be eligible for the Scheme, a business must have a taxable turnover (excluding VAT) under £150,000 per annum and a VAT-exclusive total business income below £187,500 per annum. See Notice 733 Flat-Rate Scheme for full details of eligibility.

Which sector applies to you?

The flat-rate percentages are based on historical data from various 'sectors' and reflect the average VAT paid across each sector. Under the Flat-Rate Scheme, tax paid on purchases is not recovered, and this was taken into consideration when the percentages were calculated. VAT can, however, still be reclaimed on single capital assets costing £2,000 or more (including VAT).

The HMRC website (www.hmrc.gov.uk) has a useful ready reckoner that helps you to work out what trade sector applies and therefore what flat-rate percentage you might expect.

As a sort of 'welcome gift', in your first year of VAT registration, 1% can be taken off the published flat rates until the first anniversary of registering for VAT. (So, using the reduction, a published rate of 8.5% becomes 7.5%.) After the first anniversary, the rates revert to the published level.

Joining the Scheme involves completing a very simple application form (VAT 600 FRS) available on the HMRC website, or calling the VAT National Advice Service on 0845 010 9000, which can take applications over the telephone.

8.1.5 Once registered, can you deregister?

There are a number of situations when you can apply to cancel your VAT registration. For example, if you can satisfy HMRC that:

- your taxable turnover in the next 12 months will be below the current deregistration threshold

- your tax-exclusive turnover in the past 12 months has been below the current registration threshold, or
- your turnover exceeds the registration threshold but your taxable supplies are wholly or mainly zero-rated.

There are situations in which you must deregister

You must deregister if:

- you **stop making taxable supplies**
- you **transfer your business as a going concern**, or
- you **change the legal status of your business**.

8.2 Copyright

Most of what you produce will attract copyright protection

Most of the materials you produce will be works protected by copyright. In the main, these will be classified as 'literary works'. This term covers any original written work (other than dramatic or musical work) and will include tables or compilations, computer programs, design specifications, reports and databases.

Other sorts of material you produce might attract copyright by virtue of its classification as original artistic works. For this purpose 'artistic works' are defined as including a graphic work, a photograph, a work of architecture, being a building or model for a building, or a work of artistic craftsmanship. Examples of artistic works would include diagrams, charts, maps, graphic designs and photographs.

8.2.1 Ownership

Ownership of copyright will vest in the author of the work. Section 9 of the Copyright, Designs and Patents Act 1988 (CDPA) defines 'author' as simply being the person who creates the work.

Copyright confers:

- the **moral rights to be identified as the author** of the work (the right of 'paternity')
- the **right to object to derogatory treatment of the work** (the right to 'integrity')
- the **right not to suffer false attribution**
- the **right to privacy** in respect of certain films and photographs.

These rights last for the life of the author plus 70 years (Directive 93/98 EEC).

However, even in the case of original literary or artistic works, these moral rights do not apply in all circumstances. Your expert report will, in normal circumstances, have been produced for a specific purpose and will be intended specifically for use by a third party.

8.2.2 As an employee

If employed to do forensic work, copyright will be governed by your contract of employment

If you are employed and the materials are produced in the course of your work for that employer, the employer will be the first owner of the copyright, subject to any agreement to the contrary. In those circumstances, ownership of copyright will become a matter for contract. A distinction needs to be made, however, between a contract of service and a contract for services. A contract of service will create an employer–employee relationship (essentially a contract of employment), whereas a contract for services is more likely to create a consultancy or contractor–subcontractor relationship.

Works produced in the course of employment will normally vest copyright in the employer, but there are grey areas where precise ownership might be uncertain – for example, works produced outside normal working hours or relating to projects that are unrelated to the employer or outside the scope of the employment. For this reason, it is prudent for such contracts to include a specific intellectual property rights clause.

8.2.3 As a consultant

Unless your terms set out otherwise, the copyright in your report remains with you

A more common situation for you will arise out of a contract for services where a report is commissioned from you by a third party. In the majority of cases the third party will be a party to litigation, a solicitor or the court. In those circumstances you will retain the copyright, even though the commissioning party has paid for the work and 'bought' the report or other relevant work. This presumption is, however, subject to the terms of the contract.

In many cases, it will be an express or implied term of the contract that the commissioner will be entitled to the copyright. Provided the contract is enforceable, the commissioner will, in effect, be the equitable owner of the copyright (*Lawrence Ltd -v- Aflalo* [1904] AC 17). The contract may also be construed as an assignment of the intellectual property rights or, at least, a licence to use them.

8.2.4 Photographs

Photographs are a special case

There are some specific statutory provisions that govern the copyright of commissioned photographs. The Copyright Act 1956 provides that where a person commissions a photograph, that person will, subject to certain conditions, be entitled to any subsisting copyright.

8.2.5 Contract

Spell out the copyright position in your contract

The normal assumptions of copyright ownership are, then, to some degree varied by the contractual arrangements under which the work is produced. Contractual terms can be either expressly agreed or implied from the nature of the contract. Accordingly, if you wish to retain intellectual property rights, it is important that you should spell it out in the terms and conditions of acting.

Copyright applies to physical objects, not ideas

For example, if you wish to retain the rights to publish your report or extracts from it, or to reproduce a report for teaching or training purposes, then it would be wise to expressly reserve this right when agreeing to carry out the work. Bear in mind, though, that what is being talked about here is the work itself and not the ideas it might contain. Copyright applies to the form in which those ideas are expressed – the ideas themselves are as free as air.

8.2.6 As yet uncreated work

The CDPA does permit the assignment of copyrights in works that are, as yet, uncreated. This allows flexibility when agreeing contractual terms in advance of the work being carried out.

8.2.7 Protecting your work

Nothing needs to be done to get copyright protection

If you are likely to want to claim copyright for your work, there are some basic steps you can take to protect it. UK law does not require any specific formalities to be observed, but you should take steps to:

- **identify all materials** for which copyright is likely to be claimed
- **identify yourself** as the author of the work
- **clarify any ownership and licensing** issues
- if the work has been commissioned by a third party, **ensure that there are terms in place to deal with assignment**, licensing or any implied waiver of moral rights

- **keep proper records** of the above matters and **mark any documents for which rights are claimed** in accordance with the Universal Copyright Convention, i.e. © [name of copyright owner] [year of publication].

Be aware that legal privilege can fetter your copyright freedoms

Having established copyright, however, there may be other considerations that will affect your right to the free use and publication of the material. There are, of course, issues of confidentiality (particularly in relation to medical reports). Documents that have been produced in connection with legal proceedings may also attract privilege that would be breached by disclosure or publication. You would need to give careful consideration to these and, if in doubt, seek advice.

8.2.8 Further information

The British Library advises British Library staff, members of the library profession and the general public on all aspects of copyright and copyright law. Information can be found on their website at www.bl.uk.

8.3 Retaining documents

How long should you retain documents?

The documents that are received, prepared, assessed, considered and created by you in the course of proceedings are papers of importance. A document which at the time of the original hearing might have been considered trifling could suddenly take on new importance. It is not inconceivable, therefore, that you might be asked for a document months or years after the case has been concluded.

So you are faced with a dilemma. Which documents in a case should you retain – and for how long?

8.3.1 Why retain documents at all?

There are a number of compelling reasons why you should retain papers relating to the cases in which you have been instructed.

Cases can rumble on for years

The machinery of the judicial system can be ponderous and convoluted. The tiered system of lower and upper courts, and the procedure for appeals, whether by way of case stated or rehearing, can mean that a case thought by all to be laid to rest can suddenly be reanimated. One need only look to the case of Sally Clark to see how the contents of an expert report and the expert evidence generally can be brought back before judicial scrutiny long after the original proceedings have been concluded.

Your overriding duty to the court suggests you have a duty to retain documents

Your overriding duty is owed to the court. You are required to bring to the court's attention material that might assist the court in reaching a just decision. While not expressly stated, it is suggested that this overriding duty extends beyond the life of those proceedings and so it is implicit that you should retain with reasonable care any documents upon which your opinion was founded for a reasonable time after the trial or hearing.

You also owe a duty of care to those instructing you. Again, whilst not expressly stated, it is probably implied that such duty of care extends to the safe keeping of relevant documents for a reasonable time.

Retention can also be to your own benefit

Aside from any duty owed to the court or any other party, you will have a personal interest in the retention of papers. Whilst you currently enjoy a level of immunity from suit, you are not exempt from judicial criticism or accusations of professional negligence or misconduct. Consequently, you will wish to ensure that, should you be called upon to do so, you are able to demonstrate that:

- **you complied with your duty** to the court
- **you acted in accordance with your instructions**, and
- **you reached your conclusions having exercised sound professional principles** in relation to the facts and circumstances disclosed.

In the shorter term, you may also wish to make reference to your instructions or terms of acting in the event that there is a dispute with the instructing solicitor over contractual matters – such as timely payment! So, if it is wise to retain some documents, which are they?

8.3.2 Documents sent to you

Try to return documents to the sender once the case has concluded

Probably the first question to consider is whether the document belongs to you or is the property of another. In the case of documents supplied with your instructions, the answer is simple. Wherever possible, you should seek to transfer the burden of responsibility for the retention or otherwise of these documents to those who instructed you. The instructing party will usually be better placed to assess the merits of retention and the value of individual documents to the client.

Remember, however, that in the majority of cases such documents will be copies of originals, and the solicitor may not wish to have them sent back unannounced. In the case of obviously important, original or bulky documents, it would be a sensible precaution to make enquiries of the solicitor beforehand. The solicitor might, for example, want to make his own arrangements for collection or delivery. In any event, you should take steps to ensure that vital documents are transferred safely and securely.

So, the advice is to keep separate all those documents received with instructions and to try returning them to their original source when they are no longer required.

8.3.3 Documents you generate

This leaves the following question. Which of your own documents should you retain?

Retain your instructions and terms

The most important documents to keep are those comprising your **instructions**. You should also keep on file your **terms of engagement** and **confirmation of acceptance** by the instructing solicitor. In the event that any query arises, you will want to be able to demonstrate clearly:

- the precise **nature of your instructions**
- the **issues upon which you were asked to express an opinion**
- the **nature of the information supplied** in relation to these issues, and
- the **contractual basis** on which you agreed to act.

Keep your report and correspondence

Next, you should retain:

- a **copy of your report** (including any drafts or supplements)
- **copies of correspondence** passing between you, instructing solicitors, the court or third parties, and
- **copies of any similar documents** coming into being for the purposes of the litigation.

Don't forget to back up computer-generated data

Bear in mind that relevant material might be in an electronic form and may only exist as an e-mail or other digital medium. There is probably no requirement to print these out, but it would be prudent to ensure that important information stored electronically is properly backed up.

The last (and potentially most problematic) category of documents is those you have considered or used in reaching your opinion and preparing your report. This final category may include:

- **citations**
- **extracts** from literature
- **copies of other reports**, and
- **other documents** more expressly related to the individual case and its circumstances.

Anything in the public domain need not be retained

Documents that are a matter of public record or are drawn from an existing body of literature present less of a problem than those that are not. So long as your report identifies the citations, authorities and extracts used, relied on or, in some cases, considered and rejected, there is no need to retain such extracts with the case papers. However, those documents that do not fall into this class and which have assisted you in reaching your opinion (whether they support or oppose it) should be retained.

Keep court papers that specifically mention you

Miscellaneous papers, such as copies of pleadings, copy witness statements, court orders and directions can usually be disposed of at the end of the proceedings, although it would be advisable to leave it a month or two before doing so. The exception to this would be any court papers relating specifically to you or your evidence, or those upon which you are required to act or take specific notice. While it is not your job to be the custodian of legal documents, if some question arises in relation to these documents you may be thankful to have a copy to hand.

8.3.4 Secure disposal

Always use a secure method of disposing of papers

It is, perhaps, superfluous to say that documents relating to any legal proceedings are sensitive and may be privileged or confidential. If they turn up on the municipal rubbish dump there are likely to be some embarrassing questions concerning how they arrived there. Consequently, any documents requiring disposal should be treated with discretion. The best option is to shred them.

8.4 Witness summons

A witness summons ensures the witness's attendance at court

Oral testimony is one of the bastions of our adversarial system of justice. In civil litigation, it is true, the Woolf reforms have restricted its use to some extent. But even here it remains important that parties should be able to call witnesses to testify in court and, if necessary, compel them to do so. A witness summons (formerly a subpoena) is the means provided to ensure the witness's attendance.

In civil cases, a further use of the witness summons is to secure the production of documents to the court and the attendance at a preliminary hearing of witnesses who can attest to the authenticity of the documents. This may be particularly necessary if the documents are held by a non-party and one of the litigants wishes to have sight of them before trial of the action.

Witness summonses are also a feature of criminal cases, of course, though here they are generally used to compel the attendance of witnesses whom the prosecuting authorities believe to be too frightened to give evidence voluntarily.

8.4.1 Who may be summoned, and how?

Any witness can be served with a summons

In principle, any witness who is considered competent to give evidence in a case can be compelled to attend court for that purpose. A witness is 'competent' if it is lawful for him to give evidence, and that is a matter for the judge to decide. The expert is 'compellable' if it is lawful to oblige him to give evidence, and that is governed by statute.

The competence of witnesses of fact is generally a question of whether they have sufficient understanding of the importance of the proceedings for their evidence to be heard. In the case of expert witnesses, it also involves competence in a discipline relevant to the matters in issue.

A summons requiring the attendance of a witness can only be issued by the court where the case is proceeding or where the hearing in question is to be held. The summons has to be applied for by the party needing the witness's evidence. In civil proceedings, though, the court's permission is required only if the witness is wanted for a hearing other than the trial of the action, or the trial itself is due to start in less than 7 days' time.

The issuing court can set aside a summons

Fortunately, for those on the receiving end of a summons, there is a further safeguard built into the procedure. This is that a court may, in the exercise of its discretion, rescind a summons issued previously if it can be persuaded that the summons was not sought in good faith or was oppressive in its effect. It could be, for example, that there are a number of witnesses equally competent to provide the evidence required, and the expert who has actually been summoned can make out a good case for not appearing, such as unreasonable disruption of his work.

This affords an important protection to experts – and especially, perhaps, for the better known – for they might otherwise receive all manner of speculative summonses to give evidence in cases with which they have had no prior involvement.

8.4.2 Why might an expert be summoned?

The two legitimate reasons why litigants might wish to have an expert summoned are:

- that they know, or believe, that the **expert is unwilling** to give evidence in court or produce the required documents, or
- that there is a risk the **expert may be prevented** from doing so.

It is unusual for an expert to decline to give oral evidence in a case for which instructions have been received previously, but it does happen from time to time and for a variety of reasons.

A summons can force an unwilling expert into court

It may be that the instructing solicitor has been slow in paying for the report commissioned and the expert is trying to exert pressure to settle the invoice. However, this is a tactic that can seriously backfire (see page 194).

Experts should not use payment problems as a reason not to attend court

Another reason might be that the client has indicated he/she is no longer able to pay the expert's fee for giving evidence in court. Here it is the litigant who is on weaker ground and the summons may well be set aside.

Then again, it may be that the expert is reluctant to give evidence simply because it is being sought by the opponents of the party that first instructed him. Lord Denning's famous ruling, that 'there is no property in an expert witness', was designed to put an expert in much the same position as a witness of fact. It was considered that, while communications between lawyers and experts are privileged, the court was entitled to have the facts the expert had observed adduced in evidence. Denning took the view that to allow such evidence to be excluded on grounds of privilege, or on the basis that there was a contract between the expert and the instructing party, would be contrary to public policy.

Either side can summon an expert – 'there is no property in a witness'

However, the compellability of expert witnesses in both civil and criminal proceedings is now subject to common law exceptions in cases involving experts

Legal privilege can block a witness summons

who have previously been instructed by one party or another. The courts have now ruled that an opinion can be privileged in circumstances where it is based on privileged material. Such material can be in the form of documents or merely conversations between the party and the expert.

Sometimes the summons is helpful to a busy expert

The other reason for summoning an expert is altogether much more common. It could be that the expert, though perfectly willing to give evidence, needs a summons to secure release from other duties – as happens, for example, when a police expert is required to testify on a civil matter.

A still more frequent occurrence is that the expert is working on two cases that are due to go to trial at the same time, and a clash of dates is feared. In the past, if that materialised, the solicitors concerned would have reckoned on coming to an amicable agreement whereby one of them applied for a postponement of the client's hearing to enable the expert to give evidence in both cases. In such circumstances, too, courts almost invariably agreed to one. Under the new regime of case management, however, an application of that sort is nowadays much less likely to succeed. In current circumstances, issuing a witness summons may be the only means by which a solicitor can secure priority over the expert's services for the client's benefit.

8.4.3 Practicalities

CPR and CrimPR control the use of the witness summons

The rules governing the issue of witness summonses are contained in:

- Part 34 of the CPR
- Part 28 of the CrimPR.

Part 34 of CPR may be summarised as follows.

- A witness summons is a document (Form N20) issued by a court on application from one of the parties to an action or their solicitors.
- No permission is required of the court to issue the summons – unless, that is, the trial is taking place in less than 7 days' time or attendance is being sought on a date other than that of the trial or for a hearing other than the trial.
- A court may issue a summons for proceedings before an inferior court or tribunal that lacks the power to issue one itself.
- The summons is binding on the recipient providing it is served at least 7 days before the date on which attendance is first required (although the court may waive that condition) and it remains in force for the duration of the trial or hearing, or until the judge releases the witness.
- The summons will be served by the court unless the party on whose behalf it is issued states in writing that he wishes to serve it.
- At the time of service, the witness must be offered or paid an amount to cover travelling expenses and compensation for loss of time (which sum must be stated on the summons).
- If the court is serving the summons, the party on whose behalf it is being issued must deposit this sum at the court office.

Part 28 of CrimPR may be summarised as follows.

- The court may issue or withdraw a witness summons with or without a hearing. If a hearing does take place, it must be in private, unless the court otherwise directs.
- The party applying must identify the proposed witness and explain:

  - what evidence the proposed witness can give or produce
  - why it is likely to be material evidence, and
  - why it would be in the interests of justice to issue a summons.
- A witness can be summoned to produce a document. The summons can require a witness:
  - to produce in evidence a document or thing, or
  - to give evidence about information, apparently held in confidence, that relates to another person.
- The summoned witness can object to receipt of the summons and apply to the court for it to be set aside. Possible grounds for objection include that it is not likely to be material evidence, or that, even if it is, the duties or rights of the proposed witness or of any person to whom the document or thing relates outweigh the reasons for issuing the summons.

8.4.4 Service

Service of the summons can be by post

If the court is effecting service, it will normally send the summons by first-class post. Whether or not this is appropriate will depend on the circumstances. If the witness is being summoned for 'friendly' reasons, e.g. to enable other commitments to be broken, service by post should be quite sufficient – providing, of course, it is done far enough in advance to ensure that the witness has the required notice.

If, on the other hand, the witness is believed to be unwilling to give evidence or to produce the documents sought, the solicitor initiating the procedure may elect to have the summons delivered by a process server. This will have the aim of impressing upon the witness the importance of complying with the summons and the potentially serious consequences of not doing so and being in contempt of court.

8.4.5 Payment

A properly served summons will include 'conduct money' – this is unrelated to the expert fee

As the above summary of the Rules indicates, there are two elements in the payment that witnesses are entitled to receive:

- their **travelling expenses**, and
- **compensation for their loss of time**.

The former is defined as a sum 'reasonably sufficient' to cover the cost of getting to and from the court, which is fair enough. It is the other element that is so provoking to expert witnesses.

In criminal cases, the payment scales follow MoJ guidelines

For criminal proceedings Rule 34.7(b) defines compensation for loss of time as 'such sum by way of compensation... for loss of time as may be specified in the relevant practice direction'. On consulting the Practice Direction to Part 34, one finds that it is 'to be based on the sums payable to witnesses attending the Crown Court'.

As any expert who has given evidence in a crown court will know, attendance allowances there are paid according to rates and scales fixed by the MoJ. For details, see *Appendix 9*.

In civil cases, the usual contractual terms apply

In civil cases, when a solicitor causes a witness summons to be issued, it is the solicitor, not the court, who remunerates the witness. If the summons is to be served on an expert who is happy to attend court, but who needs the summons to escape an obligation to be elsewhere, then the case of *Brown and Brown -v- Bennett and others*[1] shows that the solicitor should pay the expert whatever was agreed

1 *Brown & Brown -v- Bennett & Others* TLR 2/11/2000

previously between them for the latter's appearance in court.

The solicitor is not obliged to do that, though, if the witness has declined to give evidence for any reason, e.g. if an expert witness refuses to attend court as a tactic to exert pressure on the solicitor to pay an overdue bill. In this event, the solicitor need observe only the MoJ's rather paltry guideline figures in fixing the amount to be offered. Of course, if it should be less than the minimum they specify, the expert could apply to the court to have the summons set aside. Otherwise the expert has little option but to accept the payment. Refusing to do so does not excuse the expert from obeying the summons.

8.4.6 Setting a summons aside

The court can set aside a summons it issues

So, a court has the power to rescind any witness summons it has issued previously, and this may be done for any one of a number of reasons.

An application to have a summons set aside is made to the procedural judge in charge of the case. The judge's concern will be to determine whether the party that requested issue has abused its privilege in summoning the witness.

There are many reasons why a summons may be set aside

The summons will be set aside if, for example:

- it appears to the judge that the **request was speculative** and the party making it was merely fishing for evidence
- the judge is satisfied that the witness who had been summoned had **no evidence to give that was relevant** to the case or, if an expert witness, 'when he has **no connection with the facts or the history** of the matter'
- those serving the summons had **failed to meet the requirements concerning payment** to the

witness or, in the case of an expert, if it should appear to the court that issue of the summons had been sought to avoid having to pay the expert a previously agreed fee – as happened in the case of *Brown and Brown -v- Bennett and others.*

What is equally clear, though, is that a witness served with a summons cannot have it set aside merely by swearing that he can give no material evidence. Moreover, if it is an expert who is making the application, the judge hearing it may refuse to do as asked on the grounds that important factual information may be lost to the court should the expert not give evidence.

As Lord Justice Dunn observed in a criminal case decided in 1983, 'the court is entitled, in order to ascertain the truth, to have the actual facts which the expert has observed adduced before it'. He cited in support of this Lord Denning's judgment in a civil case 10 years previously[2]. It is implicit, too, in the CPR, both in meeting their overriding objective of enabling courts to deal with cases justly, and in respect of the duty the Rules lay on experts to help the court on matters within their expertise.

8.4.7 Penalties

Never ignore a summons; deal with it

The penalties for non-compliance with a witness summons include imprisonment for contempt of court or a fine. In addition, the expert may be ordered to pay the costs resulting from failure to attend court. Draconian punishment, indeed, that no-one in their right mind should lightly risk incurring.

2 *Seyfang -v- Searle & Co* (1973) *1 QB* 148.

9

Appendices

The content of these appendices is also accessible on-line through the Expert Library on the website of the *UK Register of Expert Witnesses*. See the introductory text to each appendix for source references.

Appendix 1: Fee rates – survey data

Since 1997, J S Publications has carried out a general expert witness survey once every 2 years. These snapshots of the expert witness landscape provide the most in-depth intelligence on expert witnesses within the UK, focusing on the work they do and their charging rates.

Presented on the following pages are the fee data for the surveys conducted between 1997 and 2007, broken down by broad discipline. For a more detailed discussion of the surveys and their data, see www.jspubs.com/Surveys/feesurveys.cfm.

Report writing	1997		1999		2001		2003		2005		2007	
	n	Hourly rate	*n*	Hourly rate	*n*	Hourly rate	*n*	Hourly rate	*n*	Hourly rate	*n*	Hourly rate
Medicine	166	£124	249	£136	200	£149	230	£153	264	£171	181	£170
Nursing, etc.	42	£76	36	£68	39	£100	42	£91	28	£104	21	£118
Engineering	116	£73	94	£71	63	£85	79	£86	84	£96	52	£112
Accountancy and Banking	34	£116	49	£135	24	£133	26	£151	34	£161	21	£174
Science and Agriculture	68	£89	79	£79	53	£78	37	£82	35	£89	19	£107
Surveying and Valuing	35	£77	49	£83	36	£104	24	£121	28	£122	18	£142
Architecture and Building	28	£75	19	£77	17	£84	27	£92	33	£97	17	£102
Others	58	£76	96	£71	50	£127	78	£109	68	£97	85	£121

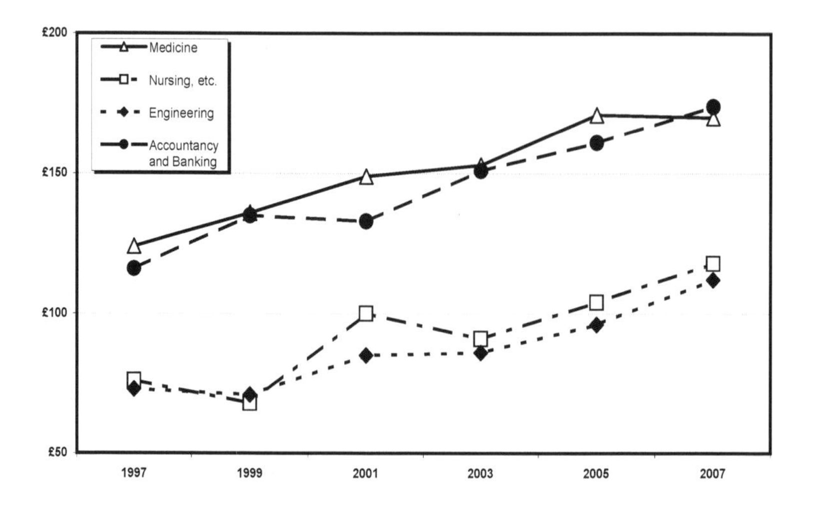

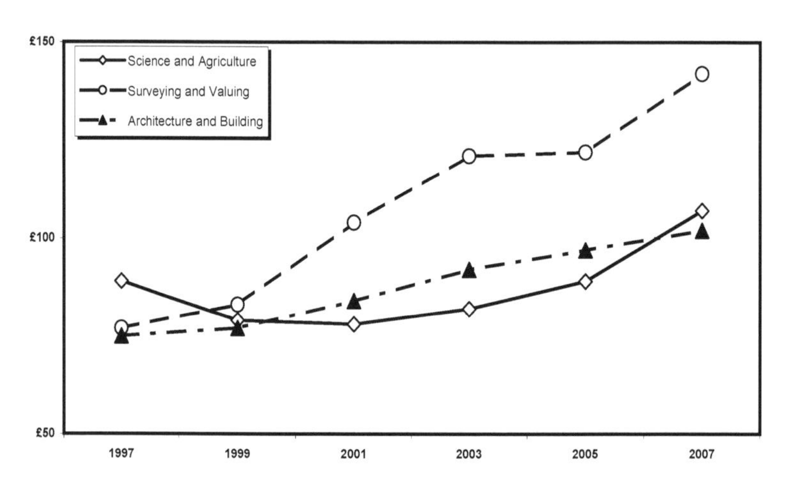

Court appearance	1997		1999		2001		2003		2005		2007	
	n	Daily rate	n	Daily rate	n	Daily rate	n	Daily rate	n	Daily rate	n	Daily rate
Medicine	166	£870	249	£890	200	£927	230	£1,041	264	£984	181	£1,163
Nursing, etc.	42	£535	36	£512	39	£718	42	£749	28	£658	21	£827
Engineering	116	£560	94	£567	63	£663	79	£694	84	£631	52	£876
Accountancy and Banking	34	£821	49	£987	24	£895	26	£1,105	34	£1,059	21	£1,105
Science and Agriculture	68	£543	79	£577	53	£648	37	£690	35	£614	19	£720
Surveying and Valuing	35	£629	49	£642	36	£787	24	£984	28	£888	18	£938
Architecture and Building	28	£612	19	£612	17	£712	27	£744	33	£610	17	£835
Others	58	£525	96	£521	50	£622	78	£802	68	£657	85	£811

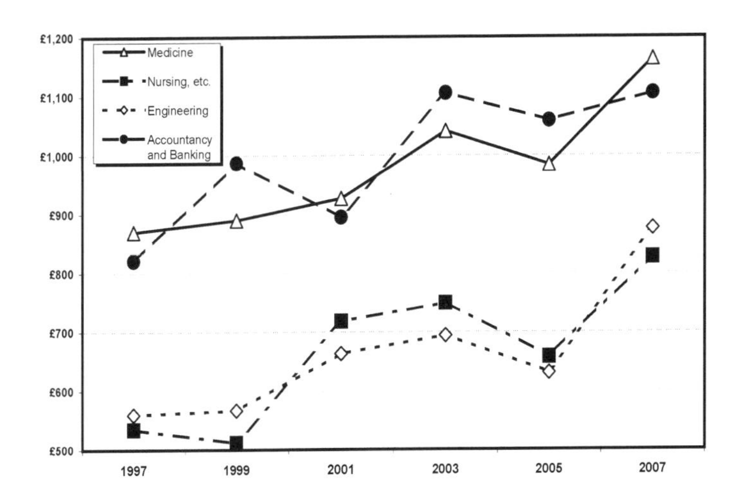

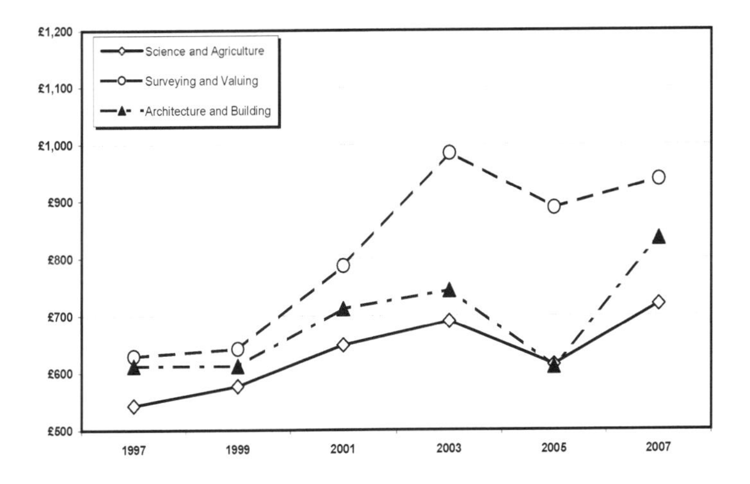

Appendix 2: Civil Procedure Rules Part 35

The following is taken from the 47th update of the CPR dated October 2008. Source: www.justice.gov.uk.

35.1 Duty to restrict expert evidence

Expert evidence shall be restricted to that which is reasonably required to resolve the proceedings.

35.2 Interpretation

A reference to an 'expert' in this Part is a reference to an expert who has been instructed to give or prepare evidence for the purpose of court proceedings.

35.3 Experts – overriding duty to the court

(1) It is the duty of an expert to help the court on the matters within his expertise.

(2) This duty overrides any obligation to the person from whom he has received instructions or by whom he is paid.

35.4 Court's power to restrict expert evidence

(1) No party may call an expert or put in evidence an expert's report without the court's permission.

(2) When a party applies for permission under this rule he must identify –

  (a) the field in which he wishes to rely on expert evidence; and

  (b) where practicable the expert in that field on whose evidence he wishes to rely.

(3) If permission is granted under this rule it shall be in relation only to the expert named or the field identified under paragraph (2).

(4) The court may limit the amount of the expert's fees and expenses that the party who wishes to rely on the expert may recover from any other party.

35.5 General requirement for expert evidence to be given in a written report

(1) Expert evidence is to be given in a written report unless the court directs otherwise.

(2) If a claim is on the fast track, the court will not direct an expert to attend a hearing unless it is necessary to do so in the interests of justice.

35.6 Written questions to experts

(1) A party may put to –

  (a) an expert instructed by another party; or

  (b) a single joint expert appointed under rule 35.7

  written questions about his report.

(2) Written questions under paragraph (1) –

  (a) may be put once only;

  (b) must be put within 28 days of service of the expert's report; and,

  (c) must be for the purpose only of clarification of the report,

  unless in any case –

    (i) the court gives permission; or

    (ii) the other party agrees.

(3) An expert's answers to questions put in accordance with paragraph (1) shall be treated as part of the expert's report.

(4) Where –

(a) a party has put a written question to an expert instructed by another party in accordance with this rule; and
(b) the expert does not answer that question,

the court may make one or both of the following orders in relation to the party who instructed the expert –

(i) that the party may not rely on the evidence of that expert; or
(ii) that the party may not recover the fees and expenses of that expert from any other party.

35.7 Court's power to direct that evidence is to be given by a single joint expert

(1) Where two or more parties wish to submit expert evidence on a particular issue, the court may direct that the evidence on that issue is to given by one expert only.
(2) The parties wishing to submit the expert evidence are called 'the instructing parties'.
(3) Where the instructing parties cannot agree who should be the expert, the court may –
(a) select the expert from a list prepared or identified by the instructing parties; or
(b) direct that the expert be selected in such other manner as the court may direct.

35.8 Instructions to a single joint expert

(1) Where the court gives a direction under rule 35.7 for a single joint expert to be used, each instructing party may give instructions to the expert.
(2) When an instructing party gives instructions to the expert he must, at the same time, send a copy of the instructions to the other instructing parties.
(3) The court may give directions about –
(a) the payment of the expert's fees and expenses; and
(b) any inspection, examination or experiments which the expert wishes to carry out.
(4) The court may, before an expert is instructed –
(a) limit the amount that can be paid by way of fees and expenses to the expert; and
(b) direct that the instructing parties pay that amount into court.
(5) Unless the court otherwise directs, the instructing parties are jointly and severally liable for the payment of the expert's fees and expenses.

35.9 Power of court to direct a party to provide information

(1) Where a party has access to information which is not reasonably available to the other party, the court may direct the party who has access to the information to –

(a) prepare and file a document recording the information; and

(b) serve a copy of that document on the other party.

35.10 Contents of report

(1) An expert's report must comply with the requirements set out in the relevant practice direction.
(2) At the end of an expert's report there must be a statement that –
(a) the expert understands his duty to the court; and
(b) he has complied with that duty.

(3) The expert's report must state the substance of all material instructions, whether written or oral, on the basis of which the report was written.

(4) The instructions referred to in paragraph (3) shall not be privileged against disclosure but the court will not, in relation to those instructions –
   (a) order disclosure of any specific document; or
   (b) permit any questioning in court, other than by the party who instructed the expert,

   unless it is satisfied that there are reasonable grounds to consider the statement of instructions given under paragraph (3) to be inaccurate or incomplete.

35.11 Use by one party of expert's report disclosed by another

(1) Where a party has disclosed an expert's report, any party may use that expert's report as evidence at the trial.

35.12 Discussions between experts

(1) The court may, at any stage, direct a discussion between experts for the purpose of requiring the experts to –
   (a) identify and discuss the expert issues in the proceedings; and
   (b) where possible, reach an agreed opinion on those issues.

(2) The court may specify the issues which the experts must discuss.

(3) The court may direct that following a discussion between the experts they must prepare a statement for the court showing –
   (a) those issues on which they agree; and
   (b) those issues on which they disagree and a summary of their reasons for disagreeing.

(4) The content of the discussion between the experts shall not be referred to at the trial unless the parties agree.

(5) Where experts reach agreement on an issue during their discussions, the agreement shall not bind the parties unless the parties expressly agree to be bound by the agreement.

35.13 Consequence of failure to disclose expert's report

(1) A party who fails to disclose an expert's report may not use the report at the trial or call the expert to give evidence orally unless the court gives permission.

35.14 Expert's right to ask court for directions

(1) An expert may file a written request for directions to assist him in carrying out his function as an expert.

(2) An expert must, unless the court orders otherwise, provide a copy of any proposed request for directions under paragraph (1) –
   (a) to the party instructing him, at least 7 days before he files the request; and
   (b) to all other parties, at least 4 days before he files it.

(3) The court, when it gives directions, may also direct that a party be served with a copy of the directions.

35.15 Assessors

(1) This rule applies where the court appoints one or more persons (an 'assessor') under section 70 of the Supreme Court Act 1981 or section 63 of the County Courts Act 1984.

(2) The assessor shall assist the court in dealing with a matter in which the assessor has skill and experience.

(3) An assessor shall take such part in the proceedings as the court may direct and in particular the court may –
   (a) direct the assessor to prepare a report for the court on any matter at issue in the proceedings; and
   (b) direct the assessor to attend the whole or any part of the trial to advise the court on any such matter.

(4) If the assessor prepares a report for the court before the trial has begun –
   (a) the court will send a copy to each of the parties; and
   (b) the parties may use it at trial.

(5) The remuneration to be paid to the assessor for his services shall be determined by the court and shall form part of the costs of the proceedings.

(6) The court may order any party to deposit in the court office a specified sum in respect of the assessor's fees and, where it does so, the assessor will not be asked to act until the sum has been deposited.

(7) Paragraphs (5) and (6) do not apply where the remuneration of the assessor is to be paid out of money provided by Parliament.

Appendix 3: Civil Procedure Rules Part 35 Practice Direction

The following is taken from the 45th update of the Rules dated October 2008. Source: www.justice.gov.uk.

Part 35 is intended to limit the use of oral expert evidence to that which is reasonably required. In addition, where possible, matters requiring expert evidence should be dealt with by a single expert. Permission of the court is always required either to call an expert or to put an expert's report in evidence. There is annexed to this Practice Direction a protocol for the instruction of experts to give evidence in civil claims. Experts and those instructing them are expected to have regard to the guidance contained in the protocol.

Expert evidence – general requirements

1.1 It is the duty of an expert to help the court on matters within his own expertise: rule 35.3(1). This duty is paramount and overrides any obligation to the person from whom the expert has received instructions or by whom he is paid: rule 35.3(2).

1.2 Expert evidence should be the independent product of the expert uninfluenced by the pressures of litigation.

1.3 An expert should assist the court by providing objective, unbiased opinion on matters within his expertise, and should not assume the role of an advocate.

1.4 An expert should consider all material facts, including those which might detract from his opinion.

1.5 An expert should make it clear:
- (a) when a question or issue falls outside his expertise; and
- (b) when he is not able to reach a definite opinion, for example because he has insufficient information.

1.6 If, after producing a report, an expert changes his view on any material matter, such change of view should be communicated to all the parties without delay, and when appropriate to the court.

Form and content of expert's reports

2.1 An expert's report should be addressed to the court and not to the party from whom the expert has received his instructions.

2.2 An expert's report must:
- (1) give details of the expert's qualifications;
- (2) give details of any literature or other material which the expert has relied on in making the report;
- (3) contain a statement setting out the substance of all facts and instructions given to the expert which are material to the opinions expressed in the report or upon which those opinions are based;
- (4) make clear which of the facts stated in the report are within the expert's own knowledge;
- (5) say who carried out any examination, measurement, test or experiment which the expert has used for the report, give the qualifications of that person, and say whether or not the test or experiment has been carried out under the expert's supervision;
- (6) where there is a range of opinion on the matters dealt with in the report –
  - (a) summarise the range of opinion, and
  - (b) give reasons for his own opinion;

(7) contain a summary of the conclusions reached;
(8) if the expert is not able to give his opinion without qualification, state the qualification; and
(9) contain a statement that the expert understands his duty to the court, and has complied and will continue to comply with that duty.

2.3 An expert's report must be verified by a statement of truth, as well as containing the statements required in paragraph 2.2 (8) and (9) above.

2.4 The form of the statement of truth is as follows: 'I confirm that insofar as the facts stated in my report are within my own knowledge I have made clear which they are and I believe them to be true, and that the opinions I have expressed represent my true and complete professional opinion.'

2.5 Attention is drawn to rule 32.14, which sets out the consequences of verifying a document containing a false statement without an honest belief in its truth. (For information about statements of truth see Part 22 and the practice direction which supplements it.)

Information

3 Under Rule 35.9 the court may direct a party with access to information which is not reasonably available to another party to serve on that other party a document which records the information. The document served must include sufficient details of all the facts, tests, experiments and assumptions which underlie any part of the information to enable the party on whom it is served to make, or to obtain, a proper interpretation of the information and an assessment of its significance.

Instructions

4 The instructions referred to in paragraph 2.2(3) will not be protected by privilege (see rule 35.10(4)). But cross-examination of the expert on the contents of his instructions will not be allowed unless the court permits it (or unless the party who gave the instructions consents to it). Before it gives permission the court must be satisfied that there are reasonable grounds to consider that the statement in the report of the substance of the instructions is inaccurate or incomplete. If the court is so satisfied, it will allow the cross-examination where it appears to be in the interests of justice to do so.

Questions to experts

5.1 Questions asked for the purpose of clarifying the expert's report (see rule 35.6) should be put, in writing, to the expert not later than 28 days after receipt of the expert's report (see paragraphs 1.2 to 1.5 above as to verification).

5.2 Where a party sends a written question or questions direct to an expert, a copy of the questions should, at the same time, be sent to the other party or parties.

5.3 The party or parties instructing the expert must pay any fees charged by that expert for answering questions put under rule 35.6. This does not affect any decision of the court as to the party who is ultimately to bear the expert's costs.

Single expert

6 Where the court has directed that the evidence on a particular issue is to be given by one expert only (rule 35.7) but there are a number of disciplines relevant to that issue, a leading expert in the dominant discipline should be identified as the single expert. He should prepare the general part of the report and be responsible

for annexing or incorporating the contents of any reports from experts in other disciplines.

Orders

6a Where an order requires an act to be done by an expert, or otherwise affects an expert, the party instructing that expert must serve a copy of the order on the expert instructed by him. In the case of a jointly instructed expert, the claimant must serve the order.

Assessors

7.1 An assessor may be appointed to assist the court under rule 35.15. Not less than 21 days before making any such appointment, the court will notify each party in writing of the name of the proposed assessor, of the matter in respect of which the assistance of the assessor will be sought and of the qualifications of the assessor to give that assistance.

7.2 Where any person has been proposed for appointment as an assessor, objection to him, either personally or in respect of his qualification, may be taken by any party.

7.3 Any such objection must be made in writing and filed with the court within 7 days of receipt of the notification referred to in paragraph 7.1 and will be taken into account by the court in deciding whether or not to make the appointment (section 63(5) of the County Courts Act 1984).

7.4 Copies of any report prepared by the assessor will be sent to each of the parties but the assessor will not give oral evidence or be open to cross-examination or questioning.

Appendix 4: Annotated CJC Experts Protocol

Source: www.jspubs.com.

The *UK Register of Expert Witnesses* is delighted that the CJC has taken the initiative – cutting through the confusion created by the regrettable inability of the Academy of Experts and Expert Witness Institute to work together – to establish a single, authoritative *Experts Protocol*. The expert witness community should welcome this development.

Having worked through the Protocol in some detail, we have identified a number of areas where further guidance may assist expert witnesses. This assertion is based upon the evidence we have gathered from our helpline, i.e. what actually troubles expert witnesses enough that they contact us. We are told, by its authors, that the Protocol cannot be modified (which seems a shame since any protocol ought to be capable of reflecting the developing needs of its constituency). We have been forced, therefore, to publish below an annotated version of the Protocol that includes these additional points of guidance. It clearly differentiates the official text from our annotations (shown in boxes).

1. Introduction

1.1 Expert witnesses perform a vital role in civil litigation. It is essential that both those who instruct experts and experts themselves are given clear guidance as to what they are expected to do in civil proceedings. The purpose of this Protocol is to provide such guidance. It has been drafted by the Civil Justice Council and reflects the rules and practice directions current [in June 2005], replacing the Code of Guidance on Expert Evidence. The authors of the Protocol wish to acknowledge the valuable assistance they obtained by drawing on earlier documents produced by the Academy of Experts and the Expert Witness Institute, as well as suggestions made by the Clinical Dispute Forum. The Protocol has been approved by the Master of the Rolls.

2. Aims of Protocol

2.1 This Protocol offers guidance to experts and to those instructing them in the interpretation of and compliance with Part 35 of the Civil Procedure Rules (CPR 35) and its associated Practice Direction (PD 35) and to further the objectives of the Civil Procedure Rules in general. It is intended to assist in the interpretation of those provisions in the interests of good practice but it does not replace them. It sets out standards for the use of experts and the conduct of experts and those who instruct them. The existence of this Protocol does not remove the need for experts and those who instruct them to be familiar with CPR35 and PD35.

2.2 Experts and those who instruct them should also bear in mind para 1.4 of the Practice Direction on Protocols which contains the following objectives, namely to:

(a) encourage the exchange of early and full information about the expert issues involved in a prospective legal claim;

(b) enable the parties to avoid or reduce the scope of litigation by agreeing the whole or part of an expert issue before commencement of proceedings; and

(c) support the efficient management of proceedings where litigation cannot be avoided.

3. Application

3.1 This Protocol applies to any steps taken for the purpose of civil proceedings by experts or those who instruct them on or after 5th September 2005.

3.2 It applies to all experts who are, or who may be, governed by CPR Part 35 and to those who instruct them. Experts are governed by Part 35 if they are or have been instructed to give or prepare evidence for the purpose of civil proceedings in a court in England and Wales (CPR 35.2).

3.3 Experts, and those instructing them, should be aware that some cases may be "specialist proceedings" (CPR 49) where there are modifications to the Civil Procedure Rules. Proceedings may also be governed by other Protocols. Further, some courts have published their own Guides which supplement the Civil Procedure Rules for proceedings in those courts. They contain provisions affecting expert evidence. Expert witnesses and those instructing them should be familiar with them when they are relevant.

3.4 Courts may take into account any failure to comply with this Protocol when making orders in relation to costs, interest, time limits, the stay of proceedings and whether to order a party to pay a sum of money into court.

Limitation

3.5 If, as a result of complying with any part of this Protocol, claims would or might be time barred under any provision in the Limitation Act 1980, or any other legislation that imposes a time limit for the bringing of an action, claimants may commence proceedings without complying with this Protocol. In such circumstances, claimants who commence proceedings without complying with all, or any part, of this Protocol must apply, giving notice to all other parties, to the court for directions as to the timetable and form of procedure to be adopted, at the same time as they request the court to issue proceedings. The court may consider whether to order a stay of the whole or part of the proceedings pending compliance with this Protocol and may make orders in relation to costs.

Privilege and Disclosure: Assume no privilege would be claimed

An expert must not be given any information that is legally privileged unless it has been decided that privilege should be waived. An expert should therefore assume that his instructions do not contain any information for which privilege would be claimed.

---

4. Duties of Experts

4.1 Experts always owe a duty to exercise reasonable skill and care to those instructing them, and to comply with any relevant professional code of ethics. However when they are instructed to give or prepare evidence for the purpose of civil proceedings in England and Wales they have an overriding duty to help the court on matters within their expertise (CPR 35.3). This duty overrides any obligation to the person instructing or paying them. Experts must not serve the exclusive interest of those who retain them.

4.2 Experts should be aware of the overriding objective that courts deal with cases justly. This includes dealing with cases proportionately, expeditiously and fairly (CPR 1.1). Experts are under an obligation to assist the court so as to enable them to deal with cases in accordance with the overriding objective. However the overriding objective does not impose on experts any duty to act as mediators between the parties or require them to trespass on the role of the court in deciding facts.

4.3 Experts should provide opinions which are independent, regardless of the pressures of litigation. In this context, a useful test of 'independence' is that the expert would express the same opinion if given the same instructions by an opposing party. Experts should not take it upon themselves to promote the point of view of the party instructing them or engage in the role of advocates.

4.4 Experts should confine their opinions to matters which are material to the disputes between the parties and provide opinions only in relation to matters which lie within their expertise. Experts should indicate without delay where particular questions or issues fall outside their expertise.

4.5 Experts should take into account all material facts before them at the time that they give their opinion. Their reports should set out those facts and any literature or any other material on which they have relied in forming their opinions. They should indicate if an opinion is provisional, or qualified, or where they consider that further information is required or if, for any other reason, they are not satisfied that an opinion can be expressed finally and without qualification.

4.6 Experts should inform those instructing them without delay of any change in their opinions on any material matter and the reason for it.

4.7 Experts should be aware that any failure by them to comply with the Civil Procedure Rules or court orders or any excessive delay for which they are responsible may result in the parties who instructed them being penalised in costs and even, in extreme cases, being debarred from placing the experts' evidence before the court. In Phillips v Symes[1] Peter Smith J held that courts may also make orders for costs (under section 51 of the Supreme Court Act 1981) directly against expert witnesses who by their evidence cause significant expense to be incurred, and do so in flagrant and reckless disregard of their duties to the Court.

5. Conduct of Experts instructed only to Advise

5.1 Part 35 only applies where experts are instructed to give opinions which are relied on for the purposes of court proceedings. Advice which the parties do not intend to adduce in litigation is likely to be confidential; the Protocol does not apply in these circumstances.[2] [3]

5.2 The same applies where, after the commencement of proceedings, experts are instructed only to advise (e.g. to comment upon a single joint expert's report) and not to give or prepare evidence for use in the proceedings.

5.3 However this Protocol does apply if experts who were formerly instructed only to advise are later instructed to give or prepare evidence for the purpose of civil proceedings.

6. The Need for Experts

6.1 Those intending to instruct experts to give or prepare evidence for the purpose of civil proceedings should consider whether expert evidence is appropriate, taking account of the principles set out in CPR Parts 1 and 35, and in particular whether:

(a) it is relevant to a matter which is in dispute between the parties;

(b) it is reasonably required to resolve the proceedings (CPR 35.1);

(c) the expert has expertise relevant to the issue on which an opinion is sought;

1 *Phillips -v- Symes* [2004] EWHC 2330 (Ch).

2 *Carlson -v- Townsend* [2001] 1 WLR 2415.

3 *Jackson -v- Marley Davenport* [2004] 1 WLR 2926.

(d) the expert has the experience, expertise and training appropriate to the value, complexity and importance of the case; and whether

(e) these objects can be achieved by the appointment of a single joint expert (see section 17 below).

6.2 Although the court's permission is not generally required to instruct an expert, the court's permission is required before experts can be called to give evidence or their evidence can be put in (CPR 35.4).

7. The Appointment of Experts

7.1 Before experts are formally instructed or the court's permission to appoint named experts is sought, the following should be established:

(a) that they have the appropriate expertise and experience;

(b) that they are familiar with the general duties of an expert;

(c) that they can produce a report, deal with questions and have discussions with other experts within a reasonable time and at a cost proportionate to the matters in issue;

(d) a description of the work required;

(e) whether they are available to attend the trial, if attendance is required; and

(f) there is no potential conflict of interest.

7.2 Terms of appointment should be agreed at the outset and should normally include:

(a) the capacity in which the expert is to be appointed (e.g. party appointed expert, single joint expert or expert advisor);

(b) the services required of the expert (e.g. provision of expert's report, answering questions in writing, attendance at meetings and attendance at court);

(c) time for delivery of the report;

(d) the basis of the expert's charges (either daily or hourly rates and an estimate of the time likely to be required, or a total fee for the services);

(e) travelling expenses and disbursements;

(f) cancellation charges;

(g) any fees for attending court;

(h) time for making the payment;

(i) whether fees are to be paid by a third party; and

(j) if a party is publicly funded, whether or not the expert's charges will be subject to assessment by a costs officer.

7.3 As to the appointment of single joint experts, see section 17 below.

7.4 When necessary, arrangements should be made for dealing with questions to experts and discussions between experts, including any directions given by the court, and provision should be made for the cost of this work.

7.5 Experts should be informed regularly about deadlines for all matters concerning them. Those instructing experts should promptly send them copies of all court orders and directions which may affect the preparation of their reports or any other matters concerning their obligations.

Conditional and contingency fees

7.6 Payments contingent upon the nature of the expert evidence given in legal proceedings, or upon the outcome of a case, must not be offered or accepted. To do so would contravene the experts' overriding duty to the court and compromise their duty of independence.

Solicitors should not offer such terms anyway
It should be remembered that the Law Society's Guide to the Professional Conduct of Solicitors specifically states at 21.11 that 'A solicitor must not make or offer to make payments to a witness contingent upon the nature of the evidence given or upon the outcome of a case'.

7.7 Agreement to delay payment of experts' fees until after the conclusion of cases is permissible as long as the amount of the fee does not depend on the outcome of the case.

8. Instructions

8.1 Those instructing experts should ensure that they give clear instructions, including the following:
  - (a) basic information, such as names, addresses, telephone numbers, dates of birth and dates of incidents;
  - (b) the nature and extent of the expertise which is called for;
  - (c) the purpose of requesting the advice or report, a description of the matter(s) to be investigated, the principal known issues and the identity of all parties;
  - (d) the statement(s) of case (if any), those documents which form part of standard disclosure and witness statements which are relevant to the advice or report;
  - (e) where proceedings have not been started, whether proceedings are being contemplated and, if so, whether the expert is asked only for advice;
  - (f) an outline programme, consistent with good case management and the expert's availability, for the completion and delivery of each stage of the expert's work; and
  - (g) where proceedings have been started, the dates of any hearings (including any Case Management Conferences and/or Pre-Trial Reviews), the name of the court, the claim number and the track to which the claim has been allocated.

8.2 Experts who do not receive clear instructions should request clarification and may indicate that they are not prepared to act unless and until such clear instructions are received.

8.3 As to the instruction of single joint experts, see section 17 below.

9. Experts' Acceptance of Instructions

9.1 Experts should confirm without delay whether or not they accept instructions. They should also inform those instructing them (whether on initial instruction or at any later stage) without delay if:
  - (a) instructions are not acceptable because, for example, they require work that falls outside their expertise, impose unrealistic deadlines, or are insufficiently clear;
  - (b) they consider that instructions are or have become insufficient to complete the work;
  - (c) they become aware that they may not be able to fulfil any of the terms of appointment;
  - (d) the instructions and/or work have, for any reason, placed them in conflict with their duties as an expert; or
  - (e) they are not satisfied that they can comply with any orders that have been made.

Obtain all relevant material

Once he has accepted instructions, the expert should request any material relevant to his consideration of the case that has not already been provided.

If a time limit has been imposed for delivery of the report, an expert's task can be made more difficult if he accepts instructions but then has to wait for a party to furnish him with missing material. For this reason, an expert may prefer to only formally accept the instruction once all the material relevant to his consideration has been delivered.

9.2 Experts must neither express an opinion outside the scope of their field of expertise, nor accept any instructions to do so.

10. Withdrawal

10.1 Where experts' instructions remain incompatible with their duties, whether through incompleteness, a conflict between their duty to the court and their instructions, or for any other substantial and significant reason, they may consider withdrawing from the case. However, experts should not withdraw without first discussing the position fully with those who instruct them and considering carefully whether it would be more appropriate to make a written request for directions from the court. If experts do withdraw, they must give formal written notice to those instructing them.

11. Experts' Right to ask Court for Directions

11.1 Experts may request directions from the court to assist them in carrying out their functions as experts. Experts should normally discuss such matters with those who instruct them before making any such request. Unless the court otherwise orders, any proposed request for directions should be copied to the party instructing the expert at least seven days before filing any request to the court, and to all other parties at least four days before filing it (CPR 35.14).

11.2 Requests to the court for directions should be made by letter, containing:

- (a) the title of the claim;
- (b) the claim number of the case;
- (c) the name of the expert;
- (d) full details of why directions are sought; and
- (e) copies of any relevant documentation.

In extremis

In very exceptional circumstances, experts may file with the court a written request for directions to assist them in carrying out their function as experts.

It is difficult to see circumstances where this course of action would be either justified or desirable from the expert's perspective. The expert works under instruction. If he has any difficulty with his instructions, he should stop working and seek clarification from those who instruct him. If they cannot resolve the problem, it is for the instructing party or parties to seek directions from the court.

---

12. Power of the Court to Direct a Party to Provide Information

12.1 If experts consider that those instructing them have not provided information which they require, they may, after discussion with those instructing them and giving notice, write to the court to seek directions (CPR 35.14).

12.2 Experts and those who instruct them should also be aware of CPR 35.9. This provides that where one party has access to information which is not readily available to the other party, the court may direct the party who has access to the information to prepare, file and copy to the other party a document recording the information. If experts require such information which has not been disclosed, they should discuss the position with those instructing them without delay, so that a request for the information can be made, and, if not forthcoming, an application can be made to the court. Unless a document appears to be essential, experts should assess the cost and time involved in the production of a document and whether its provision would be proportionate in the context of the case.

13. Contents of Experts' Reports

13.1 The content and extent of experts' reports should be governed by the scope of their instructions and general obligations, the contents of CPR 35 and PD35 and their overriding duty to the court.

13.2 In preparing reports, experts should maintain professional objectivity and impartiality at all times.

13.3 PD 35, para 2 provides that experts' reports should be addressed to the court and gives detailed directions about the form and content of such reports. All experts and those who instruct them should ensure that they are familiar with these requirements.

13.4 Model forms of Experts' Reports are available from bodies such as the Academy of Experts or the Expert Witness Institute.

13.5 Experts' reports must contain statements that they understand their duty to the court and have complied and will continue to comply with that duty (PD35 para 2.2(9)). They must also be verified by a statement of truth. The form of the statement of truth is as follows:

"*I confirm that insofar as the facts stated in my report are within my own knowledge I have made clear which they are and I believe them to be true, and that the opinions I have expressed represent my true and complete professional opinion.*"

This wording is mandatory and must not be modified.

Qualifications

13.6 The details of experts' qualifications to be given in reports should be commensurate with the nature and complexity of the case. It may be sufficient merely to state academic and professional qualifications. However, where highly specialised expertise is called for, experts should include the detail of particular training and/or experience that qualifies them to provide that highly specialised evidence.

Tests

13.7 Where tests of a scientific or technical nature have been carried out, experts should state:

(a) the methodology used; and

(b) by whom the tests were undertaken and under whose supervision, summarising their respective qualifications and experience.

Reliance on the work of others

13.8 Where experts rely in their reports on literature or other material and cite the opinions of others without having verified them, they must give details of those opinions relied on. It is likely to assist the court if the qualifications of the originator(s) are also stated.

Facts

13.9 When addressing questions of fact and opinion, experts should keep the two separate and discrete.

13.10 Experts must state those facts (whether assumed or otherwise) upon which their opinions are based. They must distinguish clearly between those facts which experts know to be true and those facts which they assume.

13.11 Where there are material facts in dispute experts should express separate opinions on each hypothesis put forward. They should not express a view in favour of one or other disputed version of the facts unless, as a result of particular expertise and experience, they consider one set of facts as being improbable or less probable, in which case they may express that view, and should give reasons for holding it.

Range of opinion

13.12 If the mandatory summary of the range of opinion is based on published sources, experts should explain those sources and, where appropriate, state the qualifications of the originator(s) of the opinions from which they differ, particularly if such opinions represent a well-established school of thought.

13.13 Where there is no available source for the range of opinion, experts may need to express opinions on what they believe to be the range which other experts would arrive at if asked. In those circumstances, experts should make it clear that the range that they summarise is based on their own judgement and explain the basis of that judgement.

Conclusions

13.14 A summary of conclusions is mandatory. The summary should be at the end of the report after all the reasoning. There may be cases, however, where the benefit to the court is heightened by placing a short summary at the beginning of the report whilst giving the full conclusions at the end. For example, it can assist with the comprehension of the analysis and with the absorption of the detailed facts if the court is told at the outset of the direction in which the report's logic will flow in cases involving highly complex matters which fall outside the general knowledge of the court.

Basis of report: material instructions

13.15 The mandatory statement of the substance of all material instructions should not be incomplete or otherwise tend to mislead. The imperative is transparency. The term "instructions" includes all material which solicitors place in front of experts in order to gain advice. The omission from the statement of 'off-the-record' oral instructions is not permitted. Courts may allow cross-examination about the instructions if there are reasonable grounds to consider that the statement may be inaccurate or incomplete.

14. After Receipt of Experts' Reports

14.1 Following the receipt of experts' reports, those instructing them should advise the experts as soon as reasonably practicable whether, and if so when, the report will be disclosed to other parties; and, if so disclosed, the date of actual disclosure.

14.2 If experts' reports are to be relied upon, and if experts are to give oral evidence, those instructing them should give the experts the opportunity to consider and comment upon other reports within their area of expertise and which deal with relevant issues at the earliest opportunity.

14.3 Those instructing experts should keep experts informed of the progress of cases, including amendments to statements of case relevant to experts' opinion.

14.4 If those instructing experts become aware of material changes in circumstances or that relevant information within their control was not previously provided to experts, they should without delay instruct experts to review, and if necessary update, the contents of their reports.

15. Amendment of Reports

15.1 It may become necessary for experts to amend their reports:

(a) as a result of an exchange of questions and answers;

(b) following agreements reached at meetings between experts; or

(c) where further evidence or documentation is disclosed.

15.2 Experts should not be asked to, and should not, amend, expand or alter any parts of reports in a manner which distorts their true opinion, but may be invited to amend or expand reports to ensure accuracy, internal consistency, completeness and relevance to the issues and clarity. Although experts should generally follow the recommendations of solicitors with regard to the form of reports, they should form their own independent views as to the opinions and contents expressed in their reports and exclude any suggestions which do not accord with their views.

15.3 Where experts change their opinion following a meeting of experts, a simple signed and dated addendum or memorandum to that effect is generally sufficient. In some cases, however, the benefit to the court of having an amended report may justify the cost of making the amendment.

15.4 Where experts significantly alter their opinion, as a result of new evidence or because evidence on which they relied has become unreliable, or for any other reason, they should amend their reports to reflect that fact. Amended reports should include reasons for amendments. In such circumstances those instructing experts should inform other parties as soon as possible of any change of opinion.

15.5 When experts intend to amend their reports, they should inform those instructing them without delay and give reasons. They should provide the amended version (or an addendum or memorandum) clearly marked as such as quickly as possible.

16. Written Questions to Experts

16.1 The procedure for putting written questions to experts (CPR 35.6) is intended to facilitate the clarification of opinions and issues after experts' reports have been served. Experts have a duty to provide answers to questions properly put. Where they fail to do so, the court may impose sanctions against the party instructing the expert, and, if, there is continued non-compliance, debar a party from relying on the report. Experts should copy their answers to those instructing them.

16.2 Experts' answers to questions automatically become part of their reports. They are covered by the statement of truth and form part of the expert evidence.

16.3 Where experts believe that questions put are not properly directed to the clarification of the report, or are disproportionate, or have been asked out of time, they should discuss the questions with those instructing them and, if appropriate, those asking the questions. Attempts should be made to resolve such problems without the need for an application to the court for directions.

Written requests for directions in relation to questions

16.4 If those instructing experts do not apply to the court in respect of questions, but experts still believe that questions are improper or out of time, experts may file written requests with the court for directions to assist in carrying out their functions as experts (CPR 35.14). See Section 11 above.

Ensuring questions have been 'properly put'
For a question to be properly put, it must conform to the requirements of Rule 35.6(2). Generally, it is for lawyers to decide whether a question meets the requirements, not experts. However, experts can avoid all possibility of censure for answering questions they ought not to have answered by relying on Rule 35.6(2)(ii). This permits any questions to be put (regardless of frequency, timing or purpose), providing all the parties agree.

If instructed by one party, an expert should send any questions he receives from another party to his instructing party and ask for permission to answer them. If permission is given, he will be covered by Rule 35.6(2)(ii).

A jointly instructed expert should only receive questions that have already been circulated to all parties, but he should nonetheless ensure all the parties agree to his answering any questions put to him.

---

17. Single Joint Experts

17.1 CPR 35 and PD35 deal extensively with the instruction and use of joint experts by the parties and the powers of the court to order their use (see CPR 35.7 and 35.8, PD35, para 5).

17.2 The Civil Procedure Rules encourage the use of joint experts. Wherever possible a joint report should be obtained. Consideration should therefore be given by all parties to the appointment of single joint experts in all cases where a court might direct such an appointment. Single joint experts are the norm in cases allocated to the small claims track and the fast track.

17.3 Where, in the early stages of a dispute, examinations, investigations, tests, site inspections, experiments, preparation of photographs, plans or other similar preliminary expert tasks are necessary, consideration should be given to the instruction of a single joint expert, especially where such matters are not, at that stage, expected to be contentious as between the parties. The objective of such an appointment should be to agree or to narrow issues.

17.5 Experts who have previously advised a party (whether in the same case or otherwise) should only be proposed as single joint experts if other parties are given all relevant information about the previous involvement.

17.6 The appointment of a single joint expert does not prevent parties from instructing their own experts to advise (but the costs of such expert advisers may not be recoverable in the case).

Joint instructions

17.7 The parties should try to agree joint instructions to single joint experts, but, in default of agreement, each party may give instructions. In particular, all parties should try to agree what documents should be included with instructions and what assumptions single joint experts should make.

17.8 Where the parties fail to agree joint instructions, they should try to agree where the areas of disagreement lie and their instructions should make this clear. If separate instructions are given, they should be copied at the same time to the other instructing parties.

17.9 Where experts are instructed by two or more parties, the terms of appointment should, unless the court has directed otherwise, or the parties have agreed otherwise, include:

(a) a statement that all the instructing parties are jointly and severally liable to pay the experts' fees and, accordingly, that experts' invoices should be sent simultaneously to all instructing parties or their solicitors (as appropriate); and

(b) a statement as to whether any order has been made limiting the amount of experts' fees and expenses (CPR 35.8(4)(a)).

17.10 Where instructions have not been received by the expert from one or more of the instructing parties the expert should give notice (normally at least 7 days) of a deadline to all instructing parties for the receipt by the expert of such instructions. Unless the instructions are received within the deadline the expert may begin work. In the event that instructions are received after the deadline but before the signing off of the report the expert should consider whether it is practicable to comply with those instructions without adversely affecting the timetable set for delivery of the report and in such a manner as to comply with the proportionality principle. An expert who decides to issue a report without taking into account instructions received after the deadline should inform the parties who may apply to the court for directions. In either event the report must show clearly that the expert did not receive instructions within the deadline, or, as the case may be, at all.

Conduct of the single joint expert

17.11 Single joint experts should keep all instructing parties informed of any material steps that they may be taking by, for example, copying all correspondence to those instructing them.

Avoid the telephone

If a jointly appointed expert is to avoid all possibility of censure, he would be wise to avoid all telephone contact with the parties, as the telephone tends to be bilateral in nature. Rely instead on written communication that can easily be copied to all parties simultaneously.

17.12 Single joint experts are Part 35 experts and so have an overriding duty to the court. They are the parties' appointed experts and therefore owe an equal duty to all parties. They should maintain independence, impartiality and transparency at all times.

17.13 Single joint experts should not attend any meeting or conference which is not a joint one, unless all the parties have agreed in writing or the court has directed that such a meeting may be held[4] and who is to pay the experts' fees for the meeting.

17.14 Single joint experts may request directions from the court – see Section 11 above.

17.15 Single joint experts should serve their reports simultaneously on all instructing parties. They should provide a single report even though they may have received instructions which contain areas of conflicting fact or allegation. If conflicting instructions lead to different opinions (for example, because the instructions require experts to make different assumptions of fact), reports may need to contain more than one set of opinions on any issue. It is for the court to determine the facts.

Cross-examination

17.16 Single joint experts do not normally give oral evidence at trial but if they do, all parties may cross-examine them. In general written questions (CPR 35.6) should

4 *Peet -v- Mid Kent Area Healthcare NHS Trust* [2002] 1 WLR 210.

be put to single joint experts before requests are made for them to attend court for the purpose of cross-examination.[5]

18. Discussions between Experts

18.1 The court has powers to direct discussions between experts for the purposes set out in the Rules (CPR 35.12). Parties may also agree that discussions take place between their experts.

18.2 Where single joint experts have been instructed but parties have, with the permission of the court, instructed their own additional Part 35 experts, there may, if the court so orders or the parties agree, be discussions between the single joint experts and the additional Part 35 experts. Such discussions should be confined to those matters within the remit of the additional Part 35 experts or as ordered by the court.

18.3 The purpose of discussions between experts should be, wherever possible, to:

(a) identify and discuss the expert issues in the proceedings;

(b) reach agreed opinions on those issues, and, if that is not possible, to narrow the issues in the case;

(c) identify those issues on which they agree and disagree and summarise their reasons for disagreement on any issue; and

(d) identify what action, if any, may be taken to resolve any of the outstanding issues between the parties.

The purpose is not negotiation

The purpose of discussions between experts is to identify, discuss and, where possible, agree opinion on expert issues. Experts should also seek to identify areas where their opinions differ, and give reasons for their disagreement. Experts should not treat the discussion as a negotiation. It is never acceptable for an expert to shift his opinion purely to obtain a concession from the other expert.

Arrangements for discussions between experts

18.4 Arrangements for discussions between experts should be proportionate to the value of cases. In small claims and fast-track cases there should not normally be meetings between experts. Where discussion is justified in such cases, telephone discussion or an exchange of letters should, in the interests of proportionality, usually suffice. In multi-track cases, discussion may be face to face, but the practicalities or the proportionality principle may require discussions to be by telephone or video conference.

18.5 The parties, their lawyers and experts should co-operate to produce the agenda for any discussion between experts, although primary responsibility for preparation of the agenda should normally lie with the parties' solicitors.

18.6 The agenda should indicate what matters have been agreed and summarise concisely those which are in issue. It is often helpful for it to include questions to be answered by the experts. If agreement cannot be reached promptly or a party is unrepresented, the court may give directions for the drawing up of the agenda. The agenda should be circulated to experts and those instructing them to allow sufficient time for the experts to prepare for the discussion.

5 *Daniels -v- Walker* [2000] 1 WLR 1382.

18.7 Those instructing experts must not instruct experts to avoid reaching agreement (or to defer doing so) on any matter within the experts' competence. Experts are not permitted to accept such instructions.

18.8 The parties' lawyers may only be present at discussions between experts if all the parties agree or the court so orders. If lawyers do attend, they should not normally intervene except to answer questions put to them by the experts or to advise about the law.[6]

18.9 The content of discussions between experts should not be referred to at trial unless the parties agree (CPR 35.12(4)). It is good practice for any such agreement to be in writing.

18.10 At the conclusion of any discussion between experts, a statement should be prepared setting out:

- (a) a list of issues that have been agreed, including, in each instance, the basis of agreement;
- (b) a list of issues that have not been agreed, including, in each instance, the basis of disagreement;
- (c) a list of any further issues that have arisen that were not included in the original agenda for discussion;
- (d) a record of further action, if any, to be taken or recommended, including as appropriate the holding of further discussions between experts.

18.11 The statement should be agreed and signed by all the parties to the discussion as soon as may be practicable.

18.12 Agreements between experts during discussions do not bind the parties unless the parties expressly agree to be bound by the agreement (CPR 35.12(5)). However, in view of the overriding objective, parties should give careful consideration before refusing to be bound by such an agreement and be able to explain their refusal should it become relevant to the issue of costs.

19. Attendance of Experts at Court

19.1 Experts instructed in cases have an obligation to attend court if called upon to do so and accordingly should ensure that those instructing them are always aware of their dates to be avoided and take all reasonable steps to be available.

19.2 Those instructing experts should:

- (a) ascertain the availability of experts before trial dates are fixed;
- (b) keep experts updated with timetables (including the dates and times experts are to attend) and the location of the court;
- (c) give consideration, where appropriate, to experts giving evidence via a video-link;
- (d) inform experts immediately if trial dates are vacated.

19.3 Experts should normally attend court without the need for the service of witness summonses, but on occasion they may be served to require attendance (CPR 34). The use of witness summonses does not affect the contractual or other obligations of the parties to pay experts' fees.

6 *Hubbard -v- Lambeth, Southwark and Lewisham HA* [2001] EWCA 1455.

Appendix 5: Criminal Procedure Rules Part 33

The following is taken from the 6th update of the Rules dated March 2008. Source: www.justice.gov.uk.

[Note. See rule 2.1(4) for the application of the rules in this Part. Part 24 contains rules about the disclosure of the substance of expert evidence. For the use of an expert report as evidence, see section 30 of the Criminal Justice Act 1988.]

33.1 Reference to expert

A reference to an 'expert' in this Part is a reference to a person who is required to give or prepare expert evidence for the purpose of criminal proceedings, including evidence required to determine fitness to plead or for the purpose of sentencing.

[Note. Expert medical evidence may be required to determine fitness to plead under section 4 of the Criminal Procedure (Insanity) Act 1964. It may be required also under section 11 of the Powers of Criminal Courts (Sentencing) Act 2000, under Part III of the Mental Health Act 1983 or under Part 12 of the Criminal Justice Act 2003. Those Acts contain requirements about the qualification of medical experts.]

33.2 Expert's duty to the court

(1) An expert must help the court to achieve the overriding objective by giving objective, unbiased opinion on matters within his expertise.

(2) This duty overrides any obligation to the person from whom he receives instructions or by whom he is paid.

(3) This duty includes an obligation to inform all parties and the court if the expert's opinion changes from that contained in a report served as evidence or given in a statement under Part 24 or Part 29.

33.3 Content of expert's report

(1) An expert's report must -
- (a) give details of the expert's qualifications, relevant experience and accreditation;
- (b) give details of any literature or other information which the expert has relied on in making the report;
- (c) contain a statement setting out the substance of all facts given to the expert which are material to the opinions expressed in the report or upon which those opinions are based;
- (d) make clear which of the facts stated in the report are within the expert's own knowledge;
- (e) say who carried out any examination, measurement, test or experiment which the expert has used for the report and,
  - (i) give the qualifications, relevant experience and accreditation of that person;
  - (ii) say whether or not the examination, measurement, test or experiment was carried out under the expert's supervision; and
  - (iii) summarise the findings on which the expert relies;
- (f) where there is a range of opinion on the matters dealt with in the report -
  - (i) summarise the range of opinion, and
  - (ii) give reasons for his own opinion;

(g) if the expert is not able to give his opinion without qualification, state the qualification;
(h) contain a summary of the conclusions reached;
(i) contain a statement that the expert understands his duty to the court, and has complied and will continue to comply with that duty; and
(j) contain the same declaration of truth as a witness statement.

(2) Only sub-paragraphs (i) and (j) of rule 33.3(1) apply to a summary by an expert of his conclusions served in advance of that expert's report.

[Note: Part 24 contains rules about the disclosure of the substance of expert evidence. Part 27 contains rules about witness statements. Declarations of truth in witness statements are required by section 9 of the Criminal Justice Act 1967 and section 5B of the Magistrates' Courts Act 1980. A party who accepts another party's expert's conclusions may admit them as facts under section 10 of the Criminal Justice Act 1967. Evidence of examinations, etc., on which an expert relies may be admissible under section 127 of the Criminal Justice Act 2003.]

33.4 Expert to be informed of service of report

A party who serves on another party or on the court a report by an expert must, at once, so inform that expert of that fact.

33.5 Pre-hearing discussion of expert evidence

(1) This rule applies where more than one party wants to introduce expert evidence.
(2) The court may direct the experts to -
(a) discuss the expert issues in the proceedings; and
(b) prepare a statement for the court of the matters on which they agree and disagree, giving their reasons.
(3) Except for that statement the content of that discussion must not be referred to without the court's permission.

33.6 Failure to comply with directions

A party may not introduce expert evidence without the court's permission if the expert has not complied with a direction under rule 33.5.

[Note. At a pre-trial hearing a court may make binding rulings about the admissibility of evidence and about questions of law under section 7 of the Criminal Justice Act 1987; sections 31 and 40 of the Criminal Procedure and Investigations Act 1996; and section 45 of the Courts Act 2003.]

33.7 Court's power to direct that evidence is to be given by a single joint expert

(1) Where more than one defendant wants to introduce expert evidence on an issue at trial, the court may direct that the evidence on that issue is to be given by one expert only.
(2) Where the co-defendants cannot agree who should be the expert, the court may –
(a) select the expert from a list prepared or identified by them; or
(b) direct that the expert be selected in such other manner as the court may direct.

33.8 Instructions to a single joint expert

(1) Where the court gives a direction under rule 33.7 for a single joint expert to be used, each of the co-defendants may give instructions to the expert.

(2) When a co-defendant gives instructions to the expert he must, at the same time, send a copy of the instructions to the other co-defendant(s).

(3) The court may give directions about –
   (a) the payment of the expert's fees and expenses; and
   (b) any examination, measurement, test or experiment which the expert wishes to carry out.

(4) The court may, before an expert is instructed, limit the amount that can be paid by way of fees and expenses to the expert.

(5) Unless the court otherwise directs, the instructing co-defendants are jointly and severally liable for the payment of the expert's fees and expenses.

Appendix 6: Practice Direction – Experts in Family Proceedings relating to Children

Source: www.justice.gov.uk.

The Practice Direction below is made by the President of the Family Division under the powers delegated to him by the Lord Chief Justice under Schedule 2, Part 1, paragraph 2(2) of the Constitutional Reform Act 2005, and is approved by the Lord Chancellor.

1. Introduction

1.1 This Practice Direction deals with the use of expert evidence and the instruction of experts in family proceedings relating to children, and comes into force on 1 April 2008. The guidance supersedes, for such proceedings, that contained in Appendix C (the Code of Guidance for Expert Witnesses in Family Proceedings) to the Protocol of June 2003 (Judicial Case Management in Public Law Children Act Cases) and in the Practice Direction to Part 17 (Experts) of the Family Procedure (Adoption) Rules 20051 ('FP(AR) 2005') with effect on and from 1 April 2008. Where the guidance refers to 'an expert' or 'the expert', this includes a reference to an expert team.

1.2 For the purposes of this guidance, the phrase 'family proceedings relating to children' is a convenient description. It is not a legal term of art and has no statutory force. In this guidance it means2:

- placement and adoption proceedings, or
- family proceedings held in private which:
  - relate to the exercise of the inherent jurisdiction of the High Court with respect to children,
  - are brought under the Children Act 1989 in any family court, or
  - are brought in the High Court and county courts and 'otherwise relate wholly or mainly to the maintenance or upbringing of a minor'.

Aims of the guidance

1.3 The guidance aims to provide the court in family proceedings relating to children with early information to determine whether an expert or expert evidence will assist the court to:

- identify, narrow and where possible agree the issues between the parties;
- provide an opinion about a question that is not within the skill and experience of the court;
- encourage the early identification of questions that need to be answered by an expert; and
- encourage disclosure of full and frank information between the parties, the court and any expert instructed.

1.4 The guidance does not aim to cover all possible eventualities. Thus it should be complied with so far as consistent in all the circumstances with the just disposal of the matter in accordance with the rules and guidance applying to the procedure in question.

Permission to instruct an expert or to use expert evidence

1.5 In family proceedings relating to children, the court's permission is required to instruct an expert. Such proceedings are confidential and, in the absence of the court's permission, disclosure of information and documents relating to such proceedings risks contravening the law of contempt of court or the various statutory provisions protecting this confidentiality. Thus, for the purposes of the law of contempt of court, information relating to such proceedings (whether or not contained in a document filed with the court or recorded in any form) may be communicated only to an expert whose instruction by a party has been permitted by the court.3 Additionally, in proceedings under the Children Act 1989, the court's permission is required to cause the child to be medically or psychiatrically examined or otherwise assessed for the purpose of the preparation of expert evidence for use in the proceedings; and, where the court's permission has not been given, no evidence arising out of such an examination or assessment may be adduced without the court's permission.4

1.6 In practice, the need to have the court's permission to disclose information or documents to an expert – and, in Children Act 1989 proceedings, to have the child examined or assessed – means that in proceedings relating to children the court strictly controls the number, fields of expertise and identity of the experts who may be first instructed and then called.

1.7 Before permission is obtained from the court to instruct an expert in family proceedings relating to children, it will be necessary for the party wishing to instruct an expert to make enquiries designed so as to provide the court with information about that expert which will enable the court to decide whether or not to give permission. In practice, enquiries may need to be made of more than one expert for this purpose. This will in turn require each expert to be given sufficient information about the case to enable that expert to decide whether or not he or she is in a position to accept instructions. Such preliminary enquiries, and the disclosure of anonymised information about the case which is a necessary part of such enquiries, will not require the court's permission and will not amount to a contempt of court: see sections 4.1 and 4.2 (Preliminary Enquiries of the Expert and Expert's Response to Preliminary Enquiries).

1.8 Section 4 (Preparation for the relevant hearing) gives guidance on applying for the court's permission to instruct an expert, and on instructing the expert, in family proceedings relating to children. The court, when granting permission to instruct an expert, will also give directions for the expert to be called to give evidence, or for the expert's report to be put in evidence: see section 4.4 (Draft Order for the relevant hearing).

When should the court be asked for permission?

1.9 The key event is 'the relevant hearing', which is any hearing at which the court's permission is sought to instruct an expert or to use expert evidence. Both expert issues should be raised with the court – and, where appropriate, with the other parties – as early as possible. This means:

- in public law proceedings under the Children Act 1989, by or at the Case Management Conference: see the Practice Direction: Guide to Case Management in Public Law Proceedings, paragraphs 13.7, 14.3 and 25(29) which contains the definition of public law proceedings for the purposes of that practice direction;
- in private law proceedings under the Children Act 1989, by or at the First Hearing Dispute Resolution Appointment: see the Private Law Programme (9 November 2004), section 4 (Process);

- in placement and adoption proceedings, by or at the First Directions Hearing: see FP(A)R 2005 rule 26 and the President's Guidance: Adoption: the New Law and Procedure (March 2006), paragraph 23.

2. General matters

Scope of the Guidance

2.1 This guidance does not apply to cases issued before 1 April 2008, but in such a case the court may direct that this guidance will apply either wholly or partly. This is subject to the overriding objective for the type of proceedings, and to the proviso that such a direction will neither cause further delay nor involve repetition of steps already taken or of decisions already made in the case.

2.2 This guidance applies to all experts who are or have been instructed to give or prepare evidence for the purpose of family proceedings relating to children in a court in England and Wales.

Pre-application instruction of experts

2.3 When experts' reports are commissioned before the commencement of proceedings, it should be made clear to the expert that he or she may in due course be reporting to the court and should therefore consider himself or herself bound by this guidance. A prospective party to family proceedings relating to children (for example, a local authority) should always write a letter of instruction when asking a potential witness for a report or an opinion, whether that request is within proceedings or pre-proceedings (for example, when commissioning specialist assessment materials, reports from a treating expert or other evidential materials); and the letter of instruction should conform to the principles set out in this guidance.

Emergency and urgent cases

2.4 In emergency or urgent cases – for example, where, before formal issue of proceedings, a without-notice application is made to the court during or out of business hours; or where, after proceedings have been issued, a previously unforeseen need for (further) expert evidence arises at short notice - a party may wish to call expert evidence without having complied with all or any part of this guidance. In such circumstances, the party wishing to call the expert evidence must apply forthwith to the court – where possible or appropriate, on notice to the other parties – for directions as to the future steps to be taken in respect of the expert evidence in question.

Orders

2.5 Where an order or direction requires an act to be done by an expert, or otherwise affects an expert, the party instructing that expert – or, in the case of a jointly instructed expert, the lead solicitor – must serve a copy of the order or direction on the expert forthwith upon receiving it.

Adults who may be protected parties

2.6 The court will investigate as soon as possible any issue as to whether an adult party or intended party to family proceedings relating to children lacks capacity (within the meaning of the Mental Capacity Act 2005) to conduct the proceedings. An adult who lacks capacity to act as a party to the proceedings is a protected party and must have a representative (a litigation friend, next friend or guardian ad litem) to conduct the proceedings on his or her behalf.

2.7 Any issue as to the capacity of an adult to conduct the proceedings must be determined before the court gives any directions relevant to that adult's role in the proceedings.

2.8 Where the adult is a protected party, his or her representative should be involved in any instruction of an expert, including the instruction of an expert to assess whether the adult, although a protected party, is competent to give evidence. The instruction of an expert is a significant step in the proceedings. The representative will wish to consider (and ask the expert to consider), if the protected party is competent to give evidence, their best interests in this regard. The representative may wish to seek advice about 'special measures'. The representative may put forward an argument on behalf of the protected party that the protected party should not give evidence.

2.9 If at any time during the proceedings there is reason to believe that a party may lack capacity to conduct the proceedings, then the court must be notified and directions sought to ensure that this issue is investigated without delay.

Child likely to lack capacity to conduct the proceedings on when he or she reaches 18

2.10 Where it appears that a child is:

- a party to the proceedings and not the subject of them;
- nearing his or her 18th birthday, and
- considered likely to lack capacity to conduct the proceedings when he or she attains the age of 18,

the court will consider giving directions for the child's capacity in this respect to be investigated.

3. The Duties of Experts

Overriding Duty

3.1 An expert in family proceedings relating to children has an overriding duty to the court that takes precedence over any obligation to the person from whom the expert has received instructions or by whom the expert is paid.

Particular Duties

3.2 Among any other duties an expert may have, an expert shall have regard to the following duties:

1) to assist the court in accordance with the overriding duty;
2) to provide advice to the court that conforms to the best practice of the expert's profession;
3) to provide an opinion that is independent of the party or parties instructing the expert;
4) to confine the opinion to matters material to the issues between the parties and in relation only to questions that are within the expert's expertise (skill and experience);
5) where a question has been put which falls outside the expert's expertise, to state this at the earliest opportunity and to volunteer an opinion as to whether another expert is required to bring expertise not possessed by those already involved or, in the rare case, as to whether a second opinion is required on

a key issue and, if possible, what questions should be asked of the second expert;

6) in expressing an opinion, to take into consideration all of the material facts including any relevant factors arising from ethnic, cultural, religious or linguistic contexts at the time the opinion is expressed;

7) to inform those instructing the expert without delay of any change in the opinion and of the reason for the change.

Content of the Expert's Report

3.3 The expert's report shall be addressed to the court and prepared and filed in accordance with the court's timetable and shall:

1) give details of the expert's qualifications and experience;

2) contain a statement setting out the substance of all material instructions (whether written or oral) summarising the facts stated and instructions given to the expert which are material to the conclusions and opinions expressed in the report;

3) identify materials that have not been produced either as original medical or other professional records or in response to an instruction from a party, as such materials may contain an assumption as to the standard of proof, the admissibility or otherwise of hearsay evidence, and other important procedural and substantive questions relating to the different purposes of other enquiries (for example, criminal or disciplinary proceedings);

4) identify all requests to third parties for disclosure and their responses in order to avoid partial disclosure which tends only to prove a case rather than give full and frank information;

5) make clear which of the facts stated in the report are within the expert's own knowledge;

6) state who carried out any test, examination or interview which the expert has used for the report and whether or not the test, examination or interview has been carried out under the expert's supervision;

7) give details of the qualifications of any person who carried out the test, examination or interview;

8) in expressing an opinion to the court:

   (a) take into consideration all of the material facts including any relevant factors arising from ethnic, cultural, religious or linguistic contexts at the time the opinion is expressed, identifying the facts, literature and any other material including research material that the expert has relied upon in forming an opinion;

   (b) describe their own professional risk assessment process and process of differential diagnosis, highlighting factual assumptions, deductions from the factual assumptions, and any unusual, contradictory or inconsistent features of the case;

   (c) highlight whether a proposition is an hypothesis (in particular a controversial hypothesis), or an opinion deduced in accordance with peer-reviewed and -tested technique, research and experience accepted as a consensus in the scientific community;

   (d) indicate whether the opinion is provisional (or qualified, as the case may be), stating the qualification and the reason for it, and identifying what further information is required to give an opinion without qualification;

9) where there is a range of opinion on any question to be answered by the expert:
   (a) summarise the range of opinion;
   (b) highlight and analyse within the range of opinion an 'unknown cause', whether on the facts of the case (for example, there is too little information to form a scientific opinion) or because of limited experience, lack of research, peer review or support in the field of expertise which the expert professes;
   (c) give reasons for any opinion expressed: the use of a balance sheet approach to the factors that support or undermine an opinion can be of great assistance to the court;
10) contain a summary of the expert's conclusions and opinions;
11) contain a statement that the expert understands his or her duty to the court and has complied and will continue to comply with that duty;
12) contain a statement that the expert:
   (a) has no conflict of interest of any kind, other than any conflict disclosed in his or her report;
   (b) does not consider that any interest disclosed affects his or her suitability as an expert witness on any issue on which he or she has given evidence;
   (c) will advise the instructing party if, between the date of the expert's report and the final hearing, there is any change in circumstances which affects the expert's answers to (a) or (b) above;
13) be verified by a statement of truth in the following form:
   'I confirm that insofar as the facts stated in my report are within my own knowledge I have made clear which they are and I believe them to be true, and that the opinions I have expressed represent my true and complete professional opinion.'

4. Preparation for the relevant hearing

Preliminary Enquiries of the Expert

4.1 In good time for the information requested to be available for the relevant hearing or for the advocates' meeting or discussion where one takes place before the relevant hearing, the solicitor for the party proposing to instruct the expert (or lead solicitor or solicitor for the child if the instruction proposed is joint) shall approach the expert with the following information:
   1) the nature of the proceedings and the issues likely to require determination by the court;
   2) the questions about which the expert is to be asked to give an opinion (including any ethnic, cultural, religious or linguistic contexts);
   3) the date when the court is to be asked to give permission for the instruction (or if - unusually - permission has already been given, the date and details of that permission);
   4) whether permission is to be asked of the court for the instruction of another expert in the same or any related field (that is, to give an opinion on the same or related questions);

5) the volume of reading which the expert will need to undertake;
6) whether or not permission has been applied for or given for the expert to examine the child;
7) whether or not it will be necessary for the expert to conduct interviews - and, if so, with whom;
8) the likely timetable of legal and social work steps;
9) when the expert's report is likely to be required;
10) whether and, if so, what date has been fixed by the court for any hearing at which the expert may be required to give evidence (in particular the Final Hearing).

It is essential that there should be proper co-ordination between the court and the expert when drawing up the case management timetable: the needs of the court should be balanced with the needs of the expert whose forensic work is undertaken as an adjunct to his or her main professional duties, whether in the National Health Service or elsewhere.

The expert should be informed at this stage of the possibility of making, through his or her instructing solicitor, representations to the court about being named or otherwise identified in any public judgment given by the court.

Expert's Response to Preliminary Enquiries

4.2 In good time for the relevant hearing or for the advocates' meeting or discussion where one takes place before the relevant hearing, the solicitors intending to instruct the expert shall obtain confirmation from the expert:

1) that acceptance of the proposed instructions will not involve the expert in any conflict of interest;
2) that the work required is within the expert's expertise;
3) that the expert is available to do the relevant work within the suggested time scale;
4) when the expert is available to give evidence, of the dates and times to avoid and, where a hearing date has not been fixed, of the amount of notice the expert will require to make arrangements to come to court (or to give evidence by video link) without undue disruption to his or her normal professional routines;
5) of the cost, including hourly or other charging rates, and likely hours to be spent, attending experts' meetings, attending court and writing the report (to include any examinations and interviews);
6) of any representations which the expert wishes to make to the court about being named or otherwise identified in any public judgment given by the court.

Where parties have not agreed on the appointment of a single joint expert before the relevant hearing, they should obtain the above confirmations in respect of all experts whom they intend to put to the court as candidates for the appointment.

The proposal to instruct an expert

4.3 Any party who proposes to ask the court for permission to instruct an expert shall, by 11 a.m. on the business day before the relevant hearing, file and serve a written proposal to instruct the expert in the following detail:

1) the name, discipline, qualifications and expertise of the expert (by way of C.V. where possible);
2) the expert's availability to undertake the work;
3) the relevance of the expert evidence sought to be adduced to the issues in the proceedings and the specific questions upon which it is proposed that the expert should give an opinion (including the relevance of any ethnic, cultural, religious or linguistic contexts);
4) the timetable for the report;
5) the responsibility for instruction;
6) whether or not the expert evidence can properly be obtained by the joint instruction of the expert by two or more of the parties;
7) whether the expert evidence can properly be obtained by only one party (for example, on behalf of the child);
8) why the expert evidence proposed cannot be given by social services undertaking a core assessment or by the Children's Guardian in accordance with their respective statutory duties;
9) the likely cost of the report on an hourly or other charging basis: where possible, the expert's terms of instruction should be made available to the court;
10) the proposed apportionment (at least in the first instance) of any jointly instructed expert's fee; when it is to be paid; and, if applicable, whether public funding has been approved.

Draft Order for the relevant hearing

4.4 Any party proposing to instruct an expert shall, by 11 a.m. on the business day before the relevant hearing, submit to the court a draft order for directions dealing in particular with:

1) the party who is to be responsible for drafting the letter of instruction and providing the documents to the expert;
2) the issues identified by the court and the questions about which the expert is to give an opinion;
3) the timetable within which the report is to be prepared, filed and served;
4) the disclosure of the report to the parties and to any other expert;
5) the organisation of, preparation for and conduct of an experts' discussion;
6) the preparation of a statement of agreement and disagreement by the experts following an experts' discussion;
7) making available to the court at an early opportunity the expert reports in electronic form;
8) the attendance of the expert at court to give oral evidence (alternatively, the expert giving his or her evidence in writing or remotely by video link), whether at or for the Final Hearing or another hearing; unless agreement about the opinions given by the expert is reached at or before the Issues Resolution Hearing ('IRH') or, if no IRH is to be held, by a specified date prior to the hearing at which the expert is to give oral evidence ('the specified date').

5. Letter of Instruction

5.1 The solicitor instructing the expert shall, within 5 business days after the relevant hearing, prepare (in agreement with the other parties where appropriate), file and serve a letter of instruction to the expert which shall:

1) set out the context in which the expert's opinion is sought (including any ethnic, cultural, religious or linguistic contexts);
2) set out the specific questions which the expert is required to answer, ensuring that they:
   (a) are within the ambit of the expert's area of expertise;
   (b) do not contain unnecessary or irrelevant detail;
   (c) are kept to a manageable number and are clear, focused and direct; and
   (d) reflect what the expert has been requested to do by the court.

   The Annex to this guidance sets out suggested questions in letters of instruction to (1) child mental health professionals or paediatricians, and (2) adult psychiatrists and applied psychologists, in Children Act 1989 proceedings;
3) list the documentation provided, or provide for the expert an indexed and paginated bundle which shall include:
   (a) a copy of the order (or those parts of the order) which gives permission for the instruction of the expert, immediately the order becomes available;
   (b) an agreed list of essential reading; and
   (c) a copy of this guidance;
4) identify materials that have not been produced either as original medical (or other professional) records or in response to an instruction from a party, as such materials may contain an assumption as to the standard of proof, the admissibility or otherwise of hearsay evidence, and other important procedural and substantive questions relating to the different purposes of other enquiries (for example, criminal or disciplinary proceedings);
5) identify all requests to third parties for disclosure and their responses, to avoid partial disclosure, which tends only to prove a case rather than give full and frank information;
6) identify the relevant people concerned with the proceedings (for example, the treating clinicians) and inform the expert of his or her right to talk to them provided that an accurate record is made of the discussions;
7) identify any other expert instructed in the proceedings and advise the expert of his or her right to talk to the other experts provided that an accurate record is made of the discussions;
8) subject to any public funding requirement for prior authority, define the contractual basis upon which the expert is retained and in particular the funding mechanism including how much the expert will be paid (an hourly rate and overall estimate should already have been obtained), when the expert will be paid, and what limitation there might be on the amount the expert can charge for the work which he or she will have to do. In cases where the parties are publicly funded, there should also be a brief explanation of the costs and expenses excluded from public funding by Funding Code criterion 1.3 and the detailed assessment process.

Asking the court to settle the letter of instruction to a joint expert

5.2 Where the court has directed that the instructions to the expert are to be contained in a jointly agreed letter and the terms of the letter cannot be agreed, any instructing party may submit to the court a written request, which must be copied to the other instructing parties, that the court settle the letter of instruction. Where possible, the written request should be set out in an e-mail to the court, preferably sent directly to the judge dealing with the proceedings (or, in the Family Proceedings Court, to the legal adviser who will forward it to the appropriate judge or justices), and be copied by e-mail to the other instructing parties. The court will settle the letter of instruction, usually without a hearing to avoid delay; and will send (where practicable, by e-mail) the settled letter to the lead solicitor for transmission forthwith to the expert, and copy it to the other instructing parties for information.

Keeping the expert up to date with new documents

5.3 As often as may be necessary, the expert should be provided promptly with a copy of any new document filed at court, together with an updated document list or bundle index.

6. The Court's control of expert evidence: consequential issues

Written Questions

6.1 Any party wishing to put written questions to an expert for the purpose of clarifying the expert's report must put the questions to the expert not later than 10 business days after receipt of the report.
The court will specify the timetable according to which the expert is to answer the written questions.

Experts' Discussion or Meeting: Purpose

6.2 By the specified date, the court may - if it has not already given such a direction - direct that the experts are to meet or communicate:

1) to identify and narrow the issues in the case;
2) where possible, to reach agreement on the expert issues;
3) to identify the reasons for disagreement on any expert question and what, if any, action needs to be taken to resolve any outstanding disagreement or question;
4) to explain or add to the evidence in order to assist the court to determine the issues;
5) to limit, wherever possible, the need for the experts to attend court to give oral evidence.

Experts' Discussion or Meeting: Arrangements

6.3 In accordance with the directions given by the court, the solicitor or other professional who is given the responsibility by the court ('the nominated professional') shall - within 15 business days after the experts' reports have been filed and copied to the other parties – make arrangements for the experts to meet or communicate. Where applicable, the following matters should be considered:

1) where permission has been given for the instruction of experts from different disciplines, a global discussion may be held relating to those questions that concern all or most of them;

2) separate discussions may have to be held among experts from the same or related disciplines, but care should be taken to ensure that the discussions complement each other so that related questions are discussed by all relevant experts;
3) 5 business days prior to a discussion or meeting, the nominated professional should formulate an agenda including a list of questions for consideration. The agenda should contain only those questions which are intended to clarify areas of agreement or disagreement. Questions which repeat questions asked in the letter of instruction or which seek to rehearse cross-examination in advance of the hearing should be rejected as likely to defeat the purpose of the meeting.
   The agenda may usefully take the form of a list of questions to be circulated among the other parties in advance. The agenda should comprise all questions that each party wishes the experts to consider. The agenda and list of questions should be sent to each of the experts not later than 2 clear business days before the discussion;
4) the nominated professional may exercise his or her discretion to accept further questions after the agenda with list of questions has been circulated to the parties. Only in exceptional circumstances should questions be added to the agenda within the 2-day period before the meeting. Under no circumstances should any question received on the day of or during the meeting be accepted. Strictness in this regard is vital, for adequate notice of the questions enables the parties to identify and isolate the issues in the case before the meeting so that the experts' discussion at the meeting can concentrate on those issues;
5) the discussion should be chaired by the nominated professional. A minute must be taken of the questions answered by the experts, and a Statement of Agreement and Disagreement must be prepared which should be agreed and signed by each of the experts who participated in the discussion. The statement should be served and filed not later than 5 business days after the discussion has taken place;
6) in each case, whether some or all of the experts participate by telephone conference or video link to ensure that minimum disruption is caused to professional schedules and that costs are minimised.

Meetings or conferences attended by a jointly instructed expert

6.4 Jointly instructed experts should not attend any meeting or conference which is not a joint one, unless all the parties have agreed in writing or the court has directed that such a meeting may be held, and it is agreed or directed who is to pay the expert's fees for the meeting or conference. Any meeting or conference attended by a jointly instructed expert should be proportionate to the case.

Court-directed meetings involving experts in public law Children Act cases

6.5 In public law Children Act proceedings, where the court gives a direction that a meeting shall take place between the local authority and any relevant named experts for the purpose of providing assistance to the local authority in the formulation of plans and proposals for the child, the meeting shall be arranged, chaired and minuted in accordance with the directions given by the court.

7. Positions of the Parties

7. Where a party refuses to be bound by an agreement that has been reached at an experts' discussion or meeting, that party must inform the court and the other parties in writing, within 10 business days after the discussion or meeting or, where an IRH is to be held, not less than 5 business days before the IRH, of his reasons for refusing to accept the agreement.

8. Arrangements for Experts to give evidence

Preparation

8.1 Where the court has directed the attendance of an expert witness, the party who is responsible for the instruction of the expert shall, by the specified date or, where an IRH is to be held, by the IRH, ensure that:

1) a date and time (if possible, convenient to the expert) are fixed for the court to hear the expert's evidence, substantially in advance of the hearing at which the expert is to give oral evidence and no later than a specified date prior to that hearing or, where an IRH is to be held, than the IRH;
2) if the expert's oral evidence is not required, the expert is notified as soon as possible;
3) the witness template accurately indicates how long the expert is likely to be giving evidence, in order to avoid the inconvenience of the expert being delayed at court;
4) consideration is given in each case to whether some or all of the experts participate by telephone conference or video link, or submit their evidence in writing, to ensure that minimum disruption is caused to professional schedules and that costs are minimised.

Experts attending Court

8.2 Where expert witnesses are to be called, all parties shall, by the specified date or, where an IRH is to be held, by the IRH, ensure that:

1) the parties' advocates have identified (whether at an advocates' meeting or by other means) the issues which the experts are to address;
2) wherever possible, a logical sequence to the evidence is arranged, with experts of the same discipline giving evidence on the same day;
3) the court is informed of any circumstance where all experts agree but a party nevertheless does not accept the agreed opinion, so that directions can be given for the proper consideration of the experts' evidence and of the party's reasons for not accepting the agreed opinion;
4) in the exceptional case the court is informed of the need for a witness summons.

9. Action after the Final Hearing

9.1 Within 10 business days after the Final Hearing, the solicitor instructing the expert shall inform the expert in writing of the outcome of the case, and of the use made by the court of the expert's opinion.

9.2 Where the court directs preparation of a transcript, it may also direct that the solicitor instructing the expert shall send a copy to the expert within 10 business days after receiving the transcript.

9.3 After a Final Hearing in the Family Proceedings Court, the (lead) solicitor instructing the expert shall send the expert a copy of the court's written reasons for its decision within 10 business days after receiving the written reasons.

Appendix 7: Terms of Engagement Framework

Appointment of [*expert's name*] as an Expert in the matter of [*case*]

Agreement made this .... day of .... 20... between [solicitor's name] (hereinafter called the Appointor) of [*firm's name and address*] and [*expert's name*] (hereinafter called the Expert) of [expert's address].

As witness the hands of the parties

I am duly authorised to sign this contract for and on behalf of [*firm's name*]

Signature of the Appointor ....

Signature of the Expert ....

This agreement has [*x*] pages.

Terms of Engagement of [expert's name] as an Expert in the matter of [*case*]

1. Recital of Appointment
[*Solicitor's name*], of Messrs [*firm's name*], has appointed [*expert's name*] to render advice and services in accordance with these Terms of Engagement.

2. Definitions
Unless the context requires otherwise:

(a) 'Appointor' means the solicitor instructing the Expert.
(b) 'Expert' means the person appointed to provide advice and services, which may include the giving of expert evidence.
(c) 'Client' means the person(s), firm, company or public body on whose behalf the Expert is being instructed.
(d) 'Assignment' means the matter(s) referred to the Expert for advice to which these Terms of Engagement apply.
(e) 'Fees' mean (in the absence of written agreement to the contrary) the reasonable charges of the Expert based on his or her normal hourly/daily rate for work of the type instructed and including VAT where applicable.
(f) 'Disbursements' mean all reasonable and appropriate costs and out-of-pocket expenses incurred by the Expert in carrying out the Assignment, including travel, refreshments and, should an overnight stay become necessary, hotel accommodation. VAT will be charged where applicable.

3. The Instructions
The Appointor will:

(a) provide the Expert with full and timely written instructions which clearly state:
 (i) whether the Expert is being instructed on the Appointor's own behalf or that of one of the parties to the dispute or as a Single Joint Expert pursuant to Civil Procedure Rule 35.7
 (ii) the purpose for which the Expert's advice and services are needed, including a description of the matter on which they are being sought
 (iii) which factual aspects of the matter may be in dispute
 (iv) whether the advice and services are to be provided in accordance solely with information supplied or will require independent investigation by the Expert
 (v) the precise kind of expertise called for
 (vi) the particular questions that are to be addressed
 (vii) whether the Expert will be expected to confer with experts instructed on behalf of other parties with a view to reaching agreement on the issues or narrowing those in dispute
 (viii) whether the Expert is to prepare a report for the advice of the Appointor and/or his Client or for use in court, and, if the latter, whether a draft version needs to be submitted first of all
 (ix) any time constraints for the provision of the advice, the production of the report, etc.
(b) provide the Expert with such basic additional information as names, addresses, telephone numbers and dates of incidents.
(c) supply the Expert with good-quality copies of all relevant documents.
(d) in the case of medical records, specify their location and identifying numbers and state whether consents for their disclosure have been given or are being obtained.

4. Obligations of the Appointor
The Appointor will:

(a) inform the Expert by whom his or her fees are to be paid and whether the Appointor needs to obtain authority to incur the estimated fees and disbursements before confirming the Expert's instructions.
(b) in legal aid cases:
 (i) notify the Expert that a funding certificate or legal aid order has been applied for, granted or amended
 (ii) apply to the Area Office of the Legal Services Commission for prior authority to incur the Expert's anticipated fees and disbursements and immediately advise the Expert should this authority be refused
 (iii) apply to the Area Office for interim payments on account to settle the Expert's invoices within the agreed time scale.
(c) in privately funded cases ensure that the Expert's fees and disbursements are paid within the agreed time scale, whether or not the Appointor has been placed in funds by the Client.
(d) respond promptly to any reasonable request from the Expert for, i.a.:
 (i) clarification of instructions already given
 (ii) further information or documents

(iii) permission to incur expense additional to that initially estimated
(iv) authority to engage others to undertake part of the assignment.

(e) not alter, or allow others to alter, the text of the Expert's report(s) in any way without the Expert's permission.

(f) give prompt written warning of every meeting or hearing that the Expert is, or may be, required to attend and immediate notification should they be cancelled.

(g) keep the Expert informed as to the progress of the case and its outcome.

(h) not use, or allow others to use, the Expert's report(s) for any purpose other than litigation in the matter on which the Appointor has sought the Expert's advice and services.

The Appointor's instructions are accepted by the Expert only upon the basis that the Appointor gives to the Expert full, timely and proper instructions, authority and information which will enable the Expert to lawfully and properly carry out the assignment and comply with the Expert's duty to the court, and that the Appointor will indemnify the Expert accordingly.

5. Obligations of the Expert

If the Expert is required to provide expert evidence, he or she becomes subject to the provisions of the [Civil Procedure Rules][Criminal Procedure Rules] that relate to experts. In such circumstances the Expert's primary duty would be to the Court and his or her evidence must be seen to be independent, objective and having no bias towards the party responsible for paying his or her fees. Subject to these overriding considerations, the Expert will:

(a) at all times, both during and after completion of the Assignment, adhere to professional boundaries of confidentiality, and raise with the Appointor any conflict between professional boundaries and Appointor instructions, if it becomes apparent.

(b) perform only those tasks for which he or she has the requisite qualifications and experience to undertake, and the resources needed to adequately fulfil them within the allotted time span.

(c) keep detailed time-sheets and records of tasks undertaken.

(d) promptly notify the Appointor of:
(i) any conflict of interest that would disqualify the Expert or render it undesirable for the Expert to have continued involvement with the case
(ii) any requirement the Expert perceives for the Appointor to employ additional expertise.

(e) endeavour to make him or herself available for all hearings, meetings or other necessary engagements for which he or she has received adequate notice.

(f) not negotiate with the opposing party or their advisers unless specifically authorised to do so by the Appointor or instructed to do so by order of the Court.

(g) if requested by the Appointor, provide before the hearing full and complete details of his or her costs to trial

(h) not without good cause discharge himself or herself from the appointment as Expert.

(i) at all times, both during and after completion of the Assignment, treat all aspects of it as confidential unless authorised by the Appointor to the contrary.

6. Intellectual Property Rights

(a) Unless otherwise agreed in writing, all legal and beneficial interest in intellectual property rights and rights of ownership in written reports, photographs, recordings, models and other original work created by the Expert relating to or developed by him or her in connection with the assignment given by the Appointor shall belong to the Expert.

(b) The Expert grants to the Appointor a non-exclusive, non-transferable licence to use the said intellectual property solely in connection with the assignment to which the instructions relate and for the duration of these terms of engagement but subject to clause 7(f) below.

7. Fees and Disbursements

In the absence of any written agreement to the contrary:

(a) the Appointor who instructs the Expert does so as principal and shall be personally responsible for payment of the Expert's fees and disbursements, whether or not the Appointor has been placed in funds by the client (or, in legal aid cases, by the Legal Services Commission), and the Appointor shall pay them in full, notwithstanding any provisions of the [Civil Procedure Rules][Criminal Procedure Rules] with regard to their amount, recoverability or otherwise, and whether or not the full amount has been allowed in any assessment of the costs of the case.

(b) Fees will be charged on a time costed basis at the Expert's hourly rate from time to time applicable and notified in writing by the Expert to the Appointor unless a fixed fee or some other basis of charging is agreed in advance and in writing between the Expert and the Appointor.

(c) The Expert may present interim invoices at such intervals as he or she considers fit and payment of each invoice will be due within [period] of its presentation, subject to any written waiver granted by the Expert in legal aid cases.

(d) The Expert reserves the right to charge to the Appointor the costs and expenses (including legal costs) of recovering late payments and to charge interest at the rate then in force pursuant to the Late Payment of Commercial Debts (Interest) Act 1998.

(e) If the Appointor does not make payment when due the Expert may, in addition, modify the payment terms so as to make all fees and disbursements payable in advance or require the Appointor to give such assurance, guarantee or undertaking as the Expert may reasonably require to secure the Appointor's payment obligations.

(f) Until payment in full has been made by the Appointor the Expert shall be entitled to retain all books, papers, reports, documents and other materials, whether or not these are the property of the Appointor and whether or not they relate to the assignment in respect of which the Expert has been instructed.

8. Cancellation Fees

The Expert shall be entitled to charge fees whenever:

(a) the Expert's time has been reserved for a specific hearing, meeting or other engagement, or

(b) specific instructions have been given to the Expert for an investigation and report and due to settlement of the matter, or for any other reason not the fault of the Expert, the reservation of time has been cancelled or the instructions withdrawn.

These fees will be calculated according to the following sliding scale:

Cancellation/withdrawal of instructions...	% of agreed fee
within **28** days of the hearing/date arranged for investigation/date report required, etc.	X
within **14** days of the hearing/date arranged for investigation/date report required, etc.	Y
within **7** days of the hearing/date arranged for investigation/date report required, etc.	Z

9. Disputed Fees

In the event of a dispute over the amount of the Expert's fees or disbursements, such sums that are not disputed shall be payable when due, irrespective of any counterclaim that may be alleged. That part which is in dispute can then be referred for resolution to a mediator acceptable to both parties or, if agreement cannot be reached, by using the services of the Centre for Dispute Resolution. In the event that the dispute is not resolved by means of negotiation or mediation, the Courts of England and Wales will have exclusive jurisdiction in relation to the dispute and its resolution.

10. Third Parties

These terms of engagement set out the rights and obligations of the Appointor and the Expert only. For the purposes of the Contracts (Rights of Third Parties) Act 1999, nothing in these terms shall be taken to confer or purport to confer any right or benefit on any third party and a third party shall have no right to the enforcement of any term contained herein.

Jurisdiction

This Contract shall be governed and construed in accordance with the laws of England and Wales, and both parties agree that subject to Clause 9 hereof the Courts of England and Wales shall have exclusive jurisdiction in determining any dispute arising herefrom.

Appendix 8: Criminal Regulations

Source: www.justice.gov.uk.

Extracted from the Prosecution of Offences Act 1985, the Costs in Criminal Cases (General) Regulations 1986, the Legal Aid Act 1988, the Legal Aid in Criminal and Care Proceedings (General) Regulations 1989 and the Legal Aid in Criminal and Care Proceedings (Costs) Regulations 1989

Prosecution of Offences Act 1985

Section 19

(3) The Lord Chancellor may by regulations make provision for the payment out of central funds, in such circumstances and in relation to such criminal proceedings as may be specified, of such sums as appear to the court to be reasonably necessary:
  (a) to compensate any witness in the proceedings... for the expense, trouble or loss of time properly incurred in or incidental to his attendance...

Costs in Criminal Cases (General) Regulations 1986[7]

Reg 16

(1) Where, in any proceedings in a criminal cause or matter in a magistrates' court, the Crown Court, a Divisional Court of the Queen's Bench Division, the Court of Appeal or the House of Lords:
  (a) a witness attends at the instance of the accused, a private prosecutor or the court...
  ... the expenses properly incurred by that witness... shall be allowed out of central funds..., unless the court directs otherwise.

(2) ... any entitlement to an allowance... shall be the same whether the witness... attends on the same day in one case or more than one case.

Reg 17

The Lord Chancellor shall, with the consent of the Treasury, determine the rates or scales of allowances payable out of central funds to witnesses...[8]

Reg 20

(1) The court may make an allowance in respect of an expert witness for attending to give expert evidence and for work in connection with its preparation of such an amount as it may consider reasonable having regard to the nature and difficulty of the case and the work necessarily involved.

---

7 These regulations were made pursuant to Section 19(3) of the 1985 Act.

8 For details of the current rates for expert witnesses, see Appendix 9: MoJ Guidance to Determining Officers.

Reg 21

(1) [An] expert witness who is necessarily absent from his place of residence overnight may be allowed a night allowance not exceeding the relevant amount.[9]

Reg 24

(1) Subject to paragraphs (2) and (3), a witness who travels to or from court by public transport (including by air) may be allowed the fare actually paid.
(2) Unless the court otherwise directs, only the second class fare shall be allowed under paragraph (1) for travel by railway by witnesses.[10]
(3) A witness who travels to or from court by air may be allowed the fare actually paid only if:
  (a) there is no reasonable alternative to travel by air and the class of fare paid was reasonable in all the circumstances; or
  (b) travel by air was more economical... taking into account any savings of time... and [their] consequent effect in reducing the amount of allowances payable under the other provisions of this Part of these Regulations and, where the air fare is not allowed, there may be allowed such amount as the court considers reasonable.
(4) A witness who travels to or from court by hired vehicle may be allowed:
  (a) the fare actually paid and any reasonable gratuity so paid in a case of urgency or where public transport is not reasonably available; or
  (b) in any other case, the amount of fare for travel by public transport.
(5) A witness who travels to or from court by private vehicle may be allowed an appropriate private vehicle allowance not exceeding the relevant amount.
(6) Where:
  (a) a witness is in the opinion of the court suffering from a serious illness; or
  (b) heavy exhibits have to be taken to court,
  the court may allow reasonable additional sums in excess of those allowed under paragraphs (1) to (5).

Legal Aid Act 1988 – Part V: Criminal Legal Aid

Section 25

(1) Where representation under this Part has been granted to any person, the costs of representing him shall be paid
  (a) by the Lord Chancellor, or
  (b) by the Board
  as the Lord Chancellor may direct ...
(3) The costs required by this section to be paid in respect of representing him shall not include any sum in respect of allowances to witnesses attending to give evidence in the proceedings... in any case where such allowances are payable under any other enactment... [11]

---

9 'Relevant amount' means an amount calculated in accordance with the rates or scales fixed under Reg 17.

10 Note, however, that determining officers have been advised by the MoJ that first-class travel would normally be appropriate for expert witnesses.

11 Principally, of course, the Prosecution of Offences Act 1985 quoted above.

Legal Aid in Criminal and Care Proceedings (General) Regulations 1989

Powers of area committee to authorise expenditure

Reg 54

(1) Where it appears to a legally assisted person's solicitor necessary for the proper conduct of proceedings in a magistrates' court or in the Crown Court for costs to be incurred under the legal aid order by any of the following steps:
 (a) obtaining a written report or opinion of one or more experts; [etc.]
 he may apply to the appropriate area committee for prior authority to do so.[12]

(2) Where an area committee authorises [the solicitor to take this step] it shall also authorise the maximum fee to be paid for any such report, opinion [etc.].

Restriction on payment

Reg 55

Where a legal aid order has been made, the legally assisted person's solicitor or counsel shall not receive or be a party to the making of any payment for work done in connection with the proceedings... except such payments as may be made:
 (a) out of the legal aid fund or by the Lord Chancellor, or
 (b) in respect of any expenses or fees incurred in:
  (i) preparing, preparing or considering any report, opinion or further evidence, whether provided by an expert witness or otherwise; or
  (ii) bespeaking transcripts of shorthand notes or tape recordings of any proceedings, including police questioning of suspects
where an application under regulation 54 for authority to incur such expenses or fees has been refused by the area committee.[13]

Legal Aid in Criminal and Care Proceedings (Costs) Regulations 1989

Reg 4A

(1) A solicitor may submit a claim to the appropriate authority for payment of a disbursement for which he has incurred liability in criminal proceedings in the Crown Court in accordance with the provisions of this regulation.

(2) A claim for payment may be made where:
 (a) a solicitor has obtained prior authority to incur expenditure of £100 or more under regulation 54(1)(a)... of the General Regulations; and
 (b) he has incurred liability for a disbursement under that authority of £100 or more.

(3) Without prejudice to regulation 7(6), a claim... shall not exceed the maximum fee authorised under the prior authority.

---

12 Note that no provision is made here or elsewhere in the Regulations for granting solicitors prior authority to incur costs in tendering oral (as distinct from written) expert evidence. This is because the Legal Services Commission is precluded from making payments to witnesses attending court by virtue of Section 25(3) of the Legal Aid Act 1985.

13 In other words, if prior authority to pay the proposed fee for an expert's report, etc., was to be refused, the solicitor would not then be prohibited from paying it out of private funds should these be available.

(4) A claim for payment under paragraph (1) may be made at any time before the solicitor submits a claim for costs under regulation 5(2).

(5) A claim under paragraph (1) shall be submitted to the appropriate authority in such form and manner as it may direct and shall be accompanied by the authority to incur expenditure and any invoices or other documents in support of the claim.

(6) The appropriate authority shall allow the disbursement subject to the limit in paragraph (3) above if it appears to have been reasonably incurred in accordance with prior authority.

(7) Where the appropriate authority allows the disbursement, it shall notify the solicitor and, where the disbursement includes the fees or charges of any person, that person, of the amount payable and shall authorise payment to the solicitor accordingly.

Reg 7

(4) No question as to the propriety of any step or act in relation to which prior authority has been obtained under regulation 54 of the General Regulations shall be raised on any determination of costs, unless the solicitor knew or ought reasonably to have known that the purpose for which the authority was given had failed or become irrelevant or unnecessary before the costs were incurred.

(5) Where costs are reasonably incurred in accordance with and subject to the limit imposed by a prior authority... no question shall be raised on any determination of costs as to the amount of the payment to be allowed...

(6) Where costs are incurred in taking any steps... for which authority may be given..., without authority to do so having been given or in excess of any fee authorised under regulation 54 of the General Regulations, payment in respect of those costs may nevertheless be allowed on a determination of costs.

Appendix 9: MoJ Guidance to Determining Officers

Source: www.hmcourts-service.gov.uk.

Reg 24, Travelling allowances

Guidance on allowances payable under Regulation 24 of *Part V of the Costs in Criminal Cases (General) Regulations 1986* published by the MoJ in the *Guide to Allowances, June 2007.*

(a) Public Transport Rate
Rate per mile with effect from 1.8.2001
Motor-cycles: 25p
Motor cars: 25p

(b) Standard Rate
Rate per mile with effect from 1.8.2001
Motor-cycles: 45p
Motor cars: 45p

(c) Passenger Supplement
First passenger: 2p
Each additional passenger: 1p

(d) Parking Fees – fees actually and reasonably incurred

(e) Pedal-cycle 20p with effect from 1.6.2005

Appendix 2: Guidance for Taxing/Determining Officers when assessing Expert Witness and other Allowances

Extracted from Appendix 2 of the Guide to Allowances under Part V of the Costs in Criminal Cases (General) Regulations 1986, as revised by the Lord Chancellor Department's Legal Aid Division in April 2003, published by the Public Legal Services Division, Department for Constitutional Affairs, in June 2005, and republished by the MoJ in June 2007.

1. As there are no prescribed scales for the remuneration of expert witnesses... [this] guidance is issued to assist taxing/determining officers by providing a point of reference on **quantum** for use when exercising their discretion in determining [claims from expert witnesses].

2. The figures are based upon allowances made throughout England and Wales. It is intended that the information will be revised annually.

3. The rate bands cover a wide [range] of skill and, in some cases, a number of different kinds of skill. They provide neither a minimum nor a maximum limit, merely a guide to the level of allowances in normal circumstances. It may be appropriate, having regard to the particular circumstances of the case, to depart from the guidance scales. Such occasions will, however, arise exceptionally.

4. In exercising their discretion, taxing/determining officers are to bear in mind that each case must be considered individually. They are to take into account all relevant circumstances surrounding the claim, including such things as the work done, the status or experience of the person doing the work, and the availability of such persons in the area of the country concerned.

5. In cases of difficulty, taxing/determining officers should seek advice from the Circuit Taxing Co-ordinator.

Schedule of Rates from 6 May 2003

1. **Consultant medical practitioner, psychiatrist, pathologist**
   Preparation (examination/report): .... £70–£100 per hour
   Attendance at court (full day) .... £346–£500
2. **Fire (assessor) and/or explosives expert**
   Preparation: .... £50–£75 per hour
   Attendance at court (full day) .... £255–£365
3. **Forensic scientist (including questioned document examiner), surveyor, accountant, engineer, medical practitioner, architect, veterinary surgeon, meteorologist**
   Preparation .... £47–£100 per hour
   Attendance at court (full day) .... £226–£490
4. **Fingerprint [expert]**
   Preparation .... £32–£52 per hour
   Attendance at court (full day) .... £153–£256

Appendix 10: Data protection principles

Source: www.opsi.gov.uk.

Data Protection Act 1998

SCHEDULE 1

1 Personal data shall be processed fairly and lawfully and, in particular, shall not be processed unless –
   (a) at least one of the conditions in Schedule 2 is met, and
   (b) in the case of sensitive personal data, at least one of the conditions in Schedule 3 is also met.

2 Personal data shall be obtained only for one or more specified and lawful purposes, and shall not be further processed in any manner incompatible with that purpose or those purposes.

3 Personal data shall be adequate, relevant and not excessive in relation to the purpose or purposes for which they are processed.

4 Personal data shall be accurate and, where necessary, kept up to date.

5 Personal data processed for any purpose or purposes shall not be kept for longer than is necessary for that purpose or those purposes.

6 Personal data shall be processed in accordance with the rights of data subjects under this Act.

7 Appropriate technical and organisational measures shall be taken against unauthorised or unlawful processing of personal data and against accidental loss or destruction of, or damage to, personal data.

8 Personal data shall not be transferred to a country or territory outside the European Economic Area unless that country or territory ensures an adequate level of protection for the rights and freedoms of data subjects in relation to the processing of personal data.

Index